D1134401

TRISTAN IN BRITTANY

BENN'S ESSEX LIBRARY

Edited by Edward G. Hawke, M.A. (Oxon.)
Published by Ernest Benn Limited,
Bouverie House, Fleet Street, London, E.C. 4
F'cap. 8vo.   Cloth, gilt back, 3s. 6d. each net.

LIST OF TITLES
(already published)

For further titles see end of book.

a great poem but it has one of the finest lines in all
poetry—

> " And Mark rewed therefor "

when the sunbeam glints on Iseult's face as she
lies sleeping by Tristram's side. And it is not at
all for unsuitableness, in the religious and moral
point of view, that one blue-pencils any share of
her lover's in the Graal Quest. It and he have
nothing whatever to do with each other. Iseult
is his Graal : he wants and attempts no other. His
remaining minglements with Arthurian stories
are superfluous but not exactly incompatible ; this
is utterly so. And indeed the original muddlers
seem to have felt it : for they turn him out in this
way or that long before the general acceptance of
defeat, the half success of Lancelot, the nearly
complete one of Bors, and the achievement of
Galahad have put an end to the matter. The
scenes with Lancelot and the pendant pictures of
the two queens are less obviously out of place :
but they are almost as superfluous. The most
excusable—and that rather as it might have been
than as it is—is the introduction of that nice but
unlucky pagan, Palamedes or Palomides, as a
rival lover to Iseult. But though she behaves
better than those who do not fully grasp her
character might expect, not nearly enough is made
of the situation to justify its being introduced at
all.

So let us turn for a page or two to the characters

perhaps rather wide reader of fiction in a good many languages ancient and modern, some results of that reading in connection with her subject.

Almost everybody who brings the slightest intelligence to this " reading of fiction " should see at once that this is a very tempting story ; and everybody who has even the slightest knowledge of mediæval literature must see that it would tempt one of the most prominent appetites of that literature—the appetite for attaching great stories to each other and sugar-castoring them with small ones. One must not utterly damn this appetite or habit : for without it the great Arthuriad itself, if not also the matters of France and Rome, would be nothing like so rich as they are. But it had its drawbacks. One of the worst of these is, as has been said, the dragging in of our story neck and heels into the Arthuriad itself.

It is just sixty-five years since I first possessed—it is all but seventy since I first read the two little volumes of the 1816 *Morte*. At the earliest date one simply took all one could get, was thankful and wanted more ; by the second something like criticism may have made itself felt. For, without being historically certain about the matter, I think I must also by then have read the English *Sir Tristrem* which, putting the muddles with " Thomas of Erceldoune " aside, is now held to have a pretty direct connection with *our* " Thomas." It is not pretty clearly. Its essential chapters or fyttes are, before all others, the combat (causes and circumstances variable *ad infinitum*) with Morolt (name *ad libitum*) ; the mission to Ireland first for medical and then for conjugal-ambassadorial purposes ; the falling in love (the philtre business is not, I think, quite essential, though in some ways advantageous) ; the escape from the consequent danger by the self-sacrifice (word applicable in an unusually full sense) of Brengwain ; the continuance of the passion and the ingratitude of Iseult to her substitute ; the discoveries (the sword-scene, though a shabby trick ethically, is aesthetically too fine to lose) ; the exile of Tristram and his marriage with the other Iseult ; the summons *in extremis* to Iseult of Ireland and its result. This result is possible to be brought about in various ways, but the ending by the death of the two lovers is as " inevitable " as the eyes of Venus are said to be by Shakerley Marmion in his rendering of Apuleius.

I have not given this sketch as a probable argument of any *Ur-Tristan* such as M. Bédier has dealt with in his excellent study of the matter, following, as it does in a way, that best of German Franco-mediævalists, Herr Kölbing. The battle of unity and plurality, original epic or original " lays," will not concern us here. The object is merely to give the reader of Miss Sayers' most enjoyable translation of what seems to be certainly *one* of the story's earliest forms, what seem, to a than third-hand), the early treatments of this *un*smoothest course of true love present themselves; while in our own days and our own tongue it has provoked from a rather cool writer as a rule the admirable outburst—

" What voices are these on the clear night air?
    What lights in the court? What steps on the
    stair? "

and from another from whom we might more expect kindling, the really magnificent overture of Mr. Swinburne's poem. As for *The Last Tournament*, the late Miss Weston demanded its utter excision and expulsion from all copies of Tennyson's works. It is not the best of the *Idylls* certainly, and by no means particularly happy as regards Tristram. But there is rather a fine thunderous atmosphere of coming evil about it, to which the general lucklessness of his story in all parts and forms lends a hand.

In speaking of " the *proper* story of Tristram and Iseult " I am not presuming to enter into any conflict or competition with the linguistic scholars who have dealt with the subject by venturing to enter into any discussions of date, style, relation between the various texts and the like. I think that, speaking from such a viewpoint as may be attained by a rather extensive study of literature, with the province of Romance rather specially frequented, one may · see this " proper " story which perhaps is the Beaumains one, that Malory had the pluck and the luck to incorporate, and which are thoroughly " well set " like jewels in gold. But even in Malory himself—much more in the French prose compilers on whom he pretty certainly relied, and whom M. Loseth has put together with rather appalling industry—the lovers of Lyonnois never seem at home in Joyeuse Garde ; all the less so, perhaps, because there are so many obvious but wholly second-rate reasons for bringing them there. The parallel-contrast with Lancelot and Guinevere ; the rivalry-friendship between the two heroes ; the opportunity, so curiously dear to the later romancers, of making Gawain almost a " felon knight " in comparison with them—all these only result in perhaps the very dullest part of the whole enormous history, or sea of histories and romances which are, or pretend to be, Arthurian.

It is, however, no part of the duty or of the intention of the present writer to deal in any detail with the somewhat less enormous but still copious enough mass of matter which the popularity of the proper story of Tristram and Iseult gathered round it from north to south and from west to east of civilised Europe. Not merely in English, French, and German, where the matter, as far as it is printed is pretty familiar to him, but in Scandinavian and (he believes) Bohemian, in Italian and Spanish (where his knowledge ranges from a little better than second to a little worse

INTRODUCTION

THE STORY OF TRISTAN AND ISEULT

OF all the stories that experienced the almost uncannily attractive powers of the great Arthurian legend in the Middle Ages, the most remarkable, in more ways than one, is that of the mainly but not wholly luckless loves of Tristan, or Tristram, Prince of Lyonnois, and Iseult (Yseult, Ysonde, Isotta, etc., all lovely but all themselves a little ill-starred in sound), Princess of Ireland. It is indeed very desirable that people should understand and remember the fact that this story has properly and essentially, nothing to do with Arthur at all, and that perhaps it would have been better if the two had been kept apart, or at most hooked on to each other as Amadis is to the Arthuriad in what one may call a purely complimentary but hardly even complementary fashion. Some of course would say, and perhaps think, something like this of the Graal story ; for them the present writer can only be sorry. Soul may divide from body, but not the Round Table from the Graal when once they had come together. And on the other hand there are minor romances, the chief of

To
M. K. P.

CONTENTS.

First Published ... ... *July* 1929

BENN'S ESSEX LIBRARY
Edited by Edward G. Hawke, M.A.

TRISTAN IN BRITTANY

Being the fragments of The
Romance of Tristan, written
in the XII century, by Thomas
the Anglo-Norman. Drawn
out of the French into the
English by Dorothy Leigh
Sayers, M.A., sometime scholar
of Somerville College, Oxford.

With an Introduction by
George Saintsbury.

LONDON: ERNEST BENN LTD.
Bouverie House, Fleet Street.

not merely of Iseult but of Tristram himself, with perhaps a few words on the only others of importance, Mark and Brengwain.

Tristram himself is rather a puzzling character; partly no doubt because he has been dragged into too many stories besides his own, partly because we do not quite know which *is* his own. He is, on one of what we may call the off-sides of him, the greatest knight next to Lancelot of the entire story in its widest range; yet M. Bédier has, I think, not without justice called him at one time, and in one situation, a coward. He adores Iseult, yet he not only marries someone else (more of that presently), but sometimes separates himself from his true mistress unnecessarily. At other times you do not know why he does what he does; there are few things in romance, though it is fairly fertile in such, which find less justification in pure reason——whatever there may be in rhyme——than his Hall or Saloon of Images. Though he is not Irish by birth there is something peculiarly Hibernian in some of his actions and in more of his speech and thought. I find it impossible to conceive a more gigantic though somehow or other romantic *bull* than the whole matter in which the (English?) Thomas evidently enjoys himself so much——the conduct and thoughts of his hero in connection with his marriage to Iseult of the White Hands. In itself it is a natural enough combat of *désir* and *vouloir*, which, difficult as they are to render, one may perhaps here take as meaning " longing " and "craving"—the first covering the more spiritual, the second the more corporal elements of Love. But Tristram's attitude to them is unique. He begins, not at all unnaturally, by a compound of intense longing *and* craving for the original Iseult, and of something like wrath because, while he can satisfy neither, she has at any rate no difficulty after a fashion with the last. Then it occurs to him that for this she has the more than excuse, the positive duty imposed on her by her marriage with Mark. This in its turn is succeeded by the brilliant idea that he can put himself in a parallel position for satisfying mere craving by marrying somebody. And unfortunately for everybody, discreditably for him, he carries this out. But no sooner has he done so than that sometimes useful but more often mischievous "ring of reminder" which plays so great a part in Romance, though the results are as different—as those, for instance, in *Guy of Warwick* and in *Parthenopex*—turns his thoughts into another course. The old "longing" returns in fullest force but refuses utterly to ally itself with a new "craving." He leaves his wife, a wife only in name.

One must of course admit that he is from his birth and by his name doomed to sorrow and suffering ; but among the means chosen by Fate or the poets to bring his sorrows and his sufferings about is the equipping him with some of the characteristics of a Blunderer. *Multum amavit ;* it was, if you admit the philtre, hardly his fault if there was anything wrong in his love, so that merciful *quia* may be said to present itself as a plea in his favour.   But he does blunder.

Iseult no doubt is even more in need of mercy. I think I have seen in some of the commentators her attempt to have Brengwain murdered dealt with as only an extreme instance of " pretty Fanny's way."   I do not think that pretty Fanny could find many more lenient judges of her ways than I am ; but really this seems going too far. Of course, besides the *quia multum amavit* itself (and to do her justice there are no signs of her ever being unfaithful to her lover even in favour of that really nice though pagan person already mentioned), she can plead other things.   As an Irish princess of early days she must have almost certainly in her blood not merely Celtic, which of itself pays not much more respect to the sixth than to the seventh commandments, but Scandinavian, which does not improve the mixture in this respect.   Gudrun's excuse or apology—

" I did the worst to him I loved the best "

is a smart piece of writing, but one would perhaps like to be on neither best nor worst terms with the lady ; and though her lovers had no doubt bored Queen Sigrid of Sweden, her plan of asking them all to dinner and setting fire to the barn they dined in, though practical and efficient, does not seem attractive.   That one might have fallen in love with Iseult, even without philtres, is quite probable, but it is rather difficult to like her. She is best when, in our own poet's form of the end of the story, she does not in the slightest degree wrangle with, rebuke or even notice her poor little namesake, but goes straight to her dead or dying lover and dies with him. You can parody or burlesque it, of course, as you can all the greatest things, but it is not the less great—perhaps the more—for that.

Some commentators, or the same, if I remember rightly, have been very angry at the degradation which Mark—" that unfortunate Cornish husband Mark," to alter in one word only a designation once applied to a fellow sufferer of his—undergoes in the later forms of the romance. He certainly begins as a King of England, and a by no means ungenerous though sadly unlucky and not very intelligent person ; and ends, as far as one can judge the chronology of the matter, as a mere duke or under-prince of Cornwall, head of a band of knights who are cowardly and treacherous like himself. It is by no means necessary that he should do so—indeed the fact is, like others, rather a sign of the *cheapening* of the romantic spirit. It provides a sort of obvious excuse for the lovers—a method of procedure for which the philtre itself offered a rather tempting suggestion. We find evidences of this cheapening in all sorts of places ; for instance, in the prayer of that more than Ernulphian curse of the Cid story, that the slayers of the

criminals may come from Galicia, not from Castille, and that the daggers of their death may be horn-handled, not silver or gold. The simple fact is that no person in Mark's situation can be given a *beau rôle* except by some extraordinary effort of genius; and that to degrade him and make him disagreeable is, though not a very artistic, an equally obvious method of creating sympathy with the lovers.

Brengwain is a very interesting person, unlucky in having been evidently dealt with in patches and left at the best to succeed, with the somewhat colourless Gouvernail, their master and mistress in a vague sort of way, and somewhat too much after the fashion of the followers who take a house of entertainment together in more modern fiction. Now although on strict moral standards Brengwain's conduct is far from being better than it should be, there is something decidedly attractive about her; she is equally clever in frustrating and magnanimous in forgiving her mistress's abominable conduct to her; it is pretty clear from Kaherdin's conduct as well as from Tristram's description that she was really beautiful; and her argument in reference to that narcotic pillow, as well as her consent to use and not to use it, show in combination both intellect and temperament. And the most curious, if rather disproportionately long sequel of quarrel between her and Iseult, if it is open to criticism in some ways, both tells us more about Brengwain than is usual about heroines of

romance in higher positions, and also, though perhaps in this matter one can only speak for oneself, makes one like her more. There is in the first and most obvious place the correct resentment of such a girl at having been made to bestow her graces on a coward. That, however, may be said to be all "in the specification"; what is not so, and is specially characteristic, is the evident boiling-up, volcano-fashion, of an older resentment at the earlier degradation and its abominably ungrateful reward. The exact bearing of her half and only half carrying out of her threats of revelation to Mark is a little puzzling in itself, but not out of keeping with what we know of her, and very Thomas-like. I wish some person of talents had told us what happened to Brengwain afterwards. The mere marriage with Gouvernail is nothing, for "damaged goods," as she might have been, from a strictly moral or merely corporal point of view, there was something quite undamaged and undamageable in the spirit of her. But her cushion or pillow would form an interesting item of that museum of the implements and paraphernalia of Romance which might be collected and arranged with some effect. One would take no liberties with sacred things; but this cushion of Brengwain's—a particularly useful object for no improper purpose as a piece of bedroom-furniture, especially on travel; the dark lantern of that foolish Partenopex; the white bear skins of *William of Palerne;* the lighted Christmas Tree of

Durmart le Gallois ; the great Charette itself, which
has much more interesting incidents connected
with it than any of the vehicles in the coach-house
of our "Victoria and Albert"; the boats of
Shalot and of Avalon ;—the catalogue might be
made quite a long one, even without including
the famous swords and horses, or requiring a not
small Zoo for dragons and lions and "bedevilled"
Fauns. But perhaps we are straying from the
path a little ; is it not the privilege and the delight
of Romance itself to stray from *any* path ? And
it is certainly time to say something about this
particular form of our story, though Miss Sayers
relieves us of the heavy part of the work.

It must have been an exceptionally tricksy spirit
who arranged and supervised the fate of this poem
of Thomas's. It is not, I have said, part of my
allotted business to give textual and manuscript
details, but the less scholastically or philologically
minded reader may be interested in the almost
uncanny fashion after which Thomas's fragment
begins only where his best follower, Gottfried
of Strasburg, leaves off ; and the more common-
place but sufficiently annoying one in which the
other followers, as they certainly seem to be, the
sagaman and the author of our own *Sir Tristram*
miss things just when we want them. In one
point we have perhaps the best of all, though it is
a small one in bulk. I do not know Norse well
enough to be a judge of it as pure poetry, but
neither in French nor German do I know anything

so good as the half-dozen lines ending with that already quoted "windfall of the Muses" which our otherwise not very poetical fellow has devoted to the central point of the whole. Of course, as this other Thomas, or whatever his name apparently was, followed the French which Miss Sayers has translated, there may have been something equally good there; but I should doubt it.

For this poet is rather a strange creature. It has, I think, been generally recognised that he is what might in these days be called statically and dynamically psychological. The wonderful indulgence in what another day would have called love-metaphysics, as to Tristram's second marriage (as we may almost call it), has been more than glanced at above; but as it deserves reading over and over to get the whole good of it, so it may be commented on more than once even in short space. You may at some moments and in some moods call it preposterous, but if you yourself have a mind capable of and accustomed to "dividing itself this way and that," you will soon recognise that it is nothing of the sort. It may take a little longer before you recover from what seems at first a tremendous blunder made just towards the end by Tristram, before you leave off even thinking that he deserved what follows for coolly remarking, when his unhappy namesake implores help to rescue his own ladylove from a ravisher, that it's rather late in the day but that he'll see what can be done next morning—as if in the interval nothing worse could happen to the object carried off than to a dinner-table or a sack of coals. It *is* rather hard to justify Tristram or Thomas here, but it is barely possible that he means to present his odd hero in one of his not previously unknown fits of distraction—fits when he is thinking of nothing but Iseult, and merely for the moment takes in the fact that there is some fighting to be done and observes that it shall be done, but that there is no particular hurry about it.

This quality certainly makes the poet at times, if not hard to understand, apt to present two or more ways of understanding. For instance, there is the incident, important in the story, of the watersplash and the remark on it to Kaherdin. Some have taken this as evidence not merely of confession, but of indignant confession of the Whitehanded One's having been defrauded of matrimonial rights. Yet it is certainly consistent with entire innocence, and there are other passages which seem to indicate that she only half understood, if she understood at all, Tristram's own apologies, though from them and possibly from them only she did understand that, in some way or other, something or other had not happened that ought to have happened. Besides points of what may be called general importance like these, there are in the few thousand verses many short passages—even single couplets or lines—which invite and have already received in many, if not in all cases, detailed examination, and which must have made the work of translation anything but easy.

The language is not particularly hard. Old French seldom is, though I seem to remember that the foundation of the Société des Anciens Textes was greeted by some Frenchmen of no small rank in letters with the same ungrateful grumbling which used to make English people speak even of Chaucer as legible with great difficulty, and of everything before Chaucer as not legible at all. But Thomas's thought, as anyone may see from what has been said already, is sometimes by no means plain sailing, and the extremely fragmentary condition of his text assists in making difficulty. I own that I am not clear myself what the whole would have been like, even with the help of his presumed followers. I do not think Cariado could have been made very interesting; and I rather doubt whether Thomas would have given us any very good fighting. What he might have done, judging from the quarrel between Brengwain and Iseult, is to have handled much more largely and made rather clearer the character of Iseult herself. For he was evidently a " character-monger " or nothing, and there are several opportunities in the part of the poem that we have not got from him, for interesting parallels to the self-debate of Tristram over the marriage with her of the White Hands.

Opinions may differ as to how much dealing we

should have had with that curious speciality which the later romancers seem to have, if not invented, developed disproportionately—the hunting craft of Tristram. This is of course a mere adjunct, at best or worst adjoined or conjoined by a play of words. The almost passionate attachment to one form of sport which characterised the upper class throughout Europe till the close of the Renaissance, and which was shared, as far as they dared and could, by the lower, naturally found its place somewhere in romance ; but there was no reason why it should be specially associated with Tristram, though somehow or other it was. He is the first, as the British Solomon was about the last, to be celebrated in English literature for cutting up a deer.

So also with the chess-playing which makes a figure in other forms of the story and which, judging from apparent derivatives, must have at least appeared in this. It is quite possible that Thomas was a chess-player. He thinks like one.

But what is amply evident, " from that which is here and that which is not," is that he devoted himself mainly if not wholly to what is the real business of the story—the love of Tristram and Iseult. There is of course love in all romances ; it is the great separating element which is in them and is not in the *chansons de geste* save charily and late. When, after each has become the other's,

they are separated themselves, Tristram (see text)
says to Iseult :

> "My most sweet lady, this I pray,
>   Never forget me any day."

and she answers :

> "Needs must our bodies sever thus,
>   But none can part our love from us."

Now, it may be said, thousands and millions of
men and women have expressed themselves in
similar fashion and *have* forgotten and severed
afterwards. But these did not so. In this all
important point they differ utterly from their
inevitable though rather undesired counterparts,
Lancelot and Guinevere. It has been said that
Tristram did not care anything about the Graal :
he cared for nothing but Iseult. Occasional
chopping up animals and moving chess pawns
cannot be said to constitute any additional devotion,
far less infidelity. Now Lancelot *is* devoted to
the Graal quest, and different from—even opposed
to—each other as these forms and objects of
devotion may be, they are of equal intensity. On
the other hand, while Iseult has certainly never
loved Mark before or after her fatal passion for
Tristram, and never gives the slightest encourage-
ment to Cariado, Palamedes or anybody else,
Guinevere is not only, as M. Paulin Paris (excellent
father of an excellent son) wickedly remarked,
"very subject to being carried off," but has, I

think, in early days certainly loved Arthur himself. She has excuses even outside the other wicked remark, not traceable to one author perhaps, that " Men can add but not substitute : women really substitute when they add." Arthur was, as we know, the reverse of blameless with his Camillas and things, and that unforgivable " false Guinevere." For all this and all this, I myself own to preferring this Queen as we have her in the original " French books " long before Malory and of course longer before any other English treatment, to Iseult. But on the love score alone (never mind the philtre) Iseult wins.

As for the demurrer against Tristram on the score of his union with Iseult of Brittany, little more need be said of that. It is a blur on his likeableness, perhaps even greater than that made by the attempt to murder Brengwain on the likeableness of Iseult ; and as such it is made worse by the conduct which, in a shabby sort of way, confirms his allegiance. But that is all.

So that if you comb or wash out the irrelevances with which, in this or that manner, to this or that extent, the various rehandlers have coloured and bolstered and fripperied the story, there remains a romance of love pure in one sense if not in another, which justifies and in a manner illustrates Mr. Swinburne's great overture. That it illustrates also the old commonplaces about love and sorrow accompanying each other need not be said.

" Right little peace they had therein, God wot "—
these two.   Except, and then with the sword always
hanging over as well as sometimes lying between
them, in the greenwood for a time.

I have said, perhaps too often, that I do not
enter into questions of literary origin and connection.   I confess that the sight of those too familiar
pedigrees, dangling down the page like strings of
sausages but not nearly so nourishing or succulent
as *good* sausages, has never delighted me in any way ;
while, speaking from my purely critical experience,
which is not very small, I seldom find them justified
or useful.   Such larger questions, too, as the
national origin, Céltic, Scandinavian, French, in
the wide sense, I also leave to those who love
them.   After all and before all, the way of a man
with a maid and the sequel thereof, are of no
country or language, being of all.   The story of
them takes colours and features no doubt in more
or less concordance with national and linguistic
peculiarities.   But there is something in literature,
as in the nature which it represents, that is outside
all this ; and there is force in the argument that
you are most likely to get at this atmosphere or
aura by going to the oldest form of poem or story
before it has been got at by men of letters—an
adulterating generation.   There does seem to be
fairly good evidence that this, which Miss Sayers
has so deftly—but at so much more cost of labour
and craftsmanship than the casual reader may
suspect—translated, is, though not in the strictest

sense original, older than any other that we have of one of the most widely disseminated, and even in a way greatest stories of the modern Western World. There must be something rather peculiarly attaching in it to have made it spread so far with so little bulk or variety in its central interest, however many attempts may have been made to enlarge and diversify it. Here, if there is incompleteness, there is no adulteration, and so—much good may it do to all good readers.

GEORGE SAINTSBURY.

TRANSLATOR'S NOTE

THE poem here translated appears from internal evidence to have been written about the middle of the twelfth century. All we know about the author is that he was called Thomas, and wrote in the Anglo-Norman dialect. The care he takes to stress the power and importance of King Mark, making him king, not of Cornwall only, but of all England ; and the glowing passage in which he sings the praise of London—" mult riche cite, meliur nad en cristiente "—make it probable that he was either an Englishman or at least attached to England by some very close link.

Whoever he may have been, Thomas was a poet of very great gifts. His verse at its best has that rare singing quality which the romance-writers of the langued'oil seldom attained. It is on an altogether different plane from the pedestrian couplets of that prolific society novelist, Chrestien de Troyes, and sometimes achieves a really lyric level of stark and moving simplicity.

Within the limits imposed upon him by the ideas and the poetic vocabulary of his day, Thomas is a thoughtful and competent psychologist. The story of Tristan appeals to him as a modern love-story; and many of the oddities and what appear to us the inconsistencies of his story are the result of his efforts to cram the old, brutal incidents of the original Tristan tradition into a twelfth-century conception of courtly behaviour. Unlike many poets of his day, he is not really interested in fights with giants, magical marvels and adventures by sea and land; he scrambles hurriedly over these incidents, to spread himself with loving care over long dialogues and monologues containing elaborate analysis of feelings, motives and problems of morality. His conception of the passion of love forms a kind of half-way house between the old feudal morality and the new and artificial " amour courtois," which was developed to such fantastic excess by later writers. The beloved woman is no longer a chattel; but she has not yet become a cult. The fatal love of Tristan and Iseult is an absorbing passion, before which every other consideration must give way; but the exasperating behaviour of the lovers conforms to the ordinary, human developments of that exasperating passion. Iseult behaves like a beast to her husband, to Brangwain, and Tristan himself; but she does not, like Guinevere, condemn her lover to banishment for the trivial misdemeanour of taking a ride in a waggon. She is human enough not to care how undignified and even degrading his method of arrival, provided she gets him. There is a kind of desperate beauty in this mutual passion, faithful through years of sin and unfaith on both sides, and careless of lies and shifts and incredible dishonour.

Probably this frank exposure of the squalid accompaniments of unlawful love damaged the poem in the eyes of contemporary French critics. Thomas's " Tristan " does not seem to have been very popular, for it has only been preserved in a few scattered fragments. It fell between two stools. There was not enough fighting and thrill in it to please the unsophisticated ; and it was not quite " nice " enough for the refined ladies and gentlemen who doted on Chrestien de Troyes. Indeed, Chrestien was so scandalised by it that he wrote " Cligès " as a kind of " anti-Tristan " ; borrowing Thomas's best passages and turning the story into a glorification of lawful matrimony. (The indignant supporters of Thomas may find some consolation in the fact that " Cligès " is probably the most tedious poem in the world.)

In other countries, however, Thomas found some people to appreciate him. A writer called Robert of Norway translated the poem into Norwegian for the benefit of King Haakon V, condensing all Thomas's favourite psychological passages ruthlessly in the process. Gottfried von Strasburg, greatest and sweetest of minnesingers, on the other hand, used it as the foundation of his own " Tristan " poem, expanding and amplifying it almost out of recognition. Eilhart d'Oberg also based a poem upon it; and so did the authors of the little "Folie Tristan" and the English "Sir Tristrem," while traces of Thomas's work are to be found half-buried in the monstrous amplifications of the Italian "Tavola Ritonda."

By comparing together these various versions and judiciously selecting those incidents and peculiarities of treatment which seem to belong to the original version of Thomas, M. Joseph Bédier—that distinguished mediævalist, who by rare good fortune combines profound scholarship with fine poetic insight—has succeeded in reconstructing the probable outlines of the lost portions of the story. From his great work (published in two volumes by the Société des Anciens Textes Français) I have, with his generous permission, prepared the brief prose sketch which links up the various fragments of the poem, so that English-speaking readers may get some sort of idea of the shape and proportions of Thomas's work as he originally wrote it. It must, however, be understood that these prose passages are very much condensed from the already condensed summary of M. Bédier. For a full appreciation of the details and subtleties of the story, the reader must be referred to M. Bédier's own delightful and intensely interesting study.

In translating the verse of Thomas, I have tried to follow the original as closely as possible; rendering couplet for couplet, where it was not in my power to give line for line. By this means,

I may hope to offer a little assistance to students of the original text in interpreting the poet's rather involved psychological arguments. This strict adherence to the text is also a safeguard against the intrusion of modern habits of thought and expression foreign to the twelfth-century mind. I have, for instance, avoided as far as possible carrying the sense over from one couplet to the next; for in Thomas's time, the French octo-syllabic couplet had not yet attained this freedom. Again, where Thomas had to make out his meaning with a limited and tentative vocabulary, I have voluntarily submitted to the same limita-tions. For example, in the important passage in which Thomas is contrasting two kinds of love— the bodily passion which he calls " voleir " and the finer and higher union of body, soul and spirit which he calls " desir "—I have rendered " voleir " by " will " and " desir " by " desire " consistently throughout, without using any of the more exact and scientific terms which we have had leisure to invent in the course of seven over-civilised centuries.

But again and again, I have been forced to do Thomas far less than justice by the extreme difficulty of translating some shatteringly simple sentence into English verse. Either the words did not mean the same thing in English, or they would not rhyme, or they would not come into the sixteen syllables of Thomas's rigid and unequiva-lenced metre. This—the translator's inevitable difficulty—accounts for many rough, crabbed or involved couplets for which Thomas is in no way responsible, and for which I can only hope to be forgiven—by Thomas and by the reader. Nevertheless, to use Thomas's own words :

> " Though here they find not all their will,
> I did the best with my poor skill,"

and I will hope that this translation may serve to introduce Thomas once again, after this long interval, to those English people with whom he felt so much at home.

My most grateful thanks are due to M. Joseph Bédier, for the chivalrous kindness with which he has permitted me to make use of his edition of the poem, as well as for his noble work of reconstruction and interpretation ; to Miss M. K. Pope of Somerville College, Oxford, who has carefully gone over the text to expunge mistranslations and obscurities ; and, last but not least, to Professor George Saintsbury, who has lent the weight of his great scholarship to my book in his delightful and entertaining introduction.

THE MANUSCRIPTS

THE whole of the earlier—and larger—portion of Thomas's poem appears to be irretrievably lost. The five manuscripts which still exist are all fragmentary, and comprise :

1. *The Cambridge Fragment :*
        vv. 1-52.

2. *The two Sneyd Fragments :*
                (a) vv. 53-940.
                (b) vv. 2319-3144.

3. *The Turin Fragment :*
                vv. 941-1096.
                vv. 1265-1518.

4. *The Strasburg Fragments :*
                (a) vv. 1097-1264.
                (b) vv. 1489-1493.
                vv. 1615-1688.
                (c) vv. 1785-1854.

5. *The Douce Fragment :*
                vv. 1268-3087.

CHAPTER ONE

THE BIRTH OF TRISTAN

THERE was once a lord in Armenye, young, brave and noble, that was called Rivalen. He held his land in fief to a rich duke of Brittany, Morgan by name. But three years after he was dubbed knight, Rivalen made war upon Morgan, and so slew his knights and ravaged his lands that at length Morgan sought to come to terms with him, and they arranged a truce for a time.

Now, shortly after this, Rivalen wished to cross the sea to visit foreign lands, and learn new virtues of chivalry among knights of high renown. So he confided the care of his lands to his marshal, a faithful man called Roald le Foytenant.

Rivalen had often heard tell of England, as of a country great and fair and blessed of God, rich in strong castles, flourishing towns, wide forests filled with game, in gold and silver and precious metals and furs of vair and sable. But chiefly he desired to see with his own eyes the famous knights and the courteous and hospitable people of England, and to learn their noble customs and their manner of fighting and jousting.

Above all, Rivalen had heard men praise the young king of England, King Mark of Cornwall. Mark at this time reigned over the joint kingdom of Cornwall and England. Cornwall was his hereditary fief. England became his in the following manner. When the Saxons chased out the Britons and divided the country among themselves, each one wanted to be king in his own little domain. But as this led to many disastrous quarrels, they placed themselves and their lands all under the suzerainty of Mark. And history says that they served him faithfully and he ruled them well.

So Rivalen took ship to England, and hearing that Mark was at his palace of Tintagel in Cornwall, he landed there.

Tintagel was a fair and strong castle, its tower looked out upon the sea. Giants builded it of old. All its stones were marble and its walls chequered with sinople and azure. Two watchmen guarded the gate.

When Rivalen and his companions were a little way off, they got down from horse and entered the hall courteously, two by two, robed in rich robes and holding hands. Mark greeted them honourably and made them sit at his table, and they lived with him in great joy and honour.

Now when they had sojourned there many days, Mark held a court at Tintagel. He sent letters under his seal, bidding all the great barons from all over the country to come with their wives, their sons and their daughters. Tents of rich colours

were set up in a fair wide plain, and there they held
feast, and many noble youths were dubbed knights;
and after the feast they went forth to the plain to
hold a tourney under the eyes of their ladies.
Among them all, Rivalen excelled in valour and
courtesy, so that all the ladies cried: "Ah! see
the brave knight! How nobly he bears himself!
Happy the maiden who should win his love!"

Now King Mark had a sister named Blancheflor,
so beautiful, wise and kind that her praise was sung
in many distant lands. And when she looked on
Rivalen, she loved him. "Alas!" she said to
herself, "is he an enchanter that hath so bewitched
me? for I am in torment because of him."

At the end of the tourney, Rivalen passed close
beside her, and he saluted her courteously:

"God save thee, lady fair," he said.
"Gramercy, sir," replied the maid.

From that hour, Rivalen loved Blancheflor as
much as she loved him. And after a little while
they met privately and discovered each to other
their mutual love; but Rivalen dared not openly
ask King Mark for his sister's hand, lest it should
seem presumption in a young foreign knight, so
newly come to court. Nevertheless, Mark wondered to see Rivalen remain so long in England,
and began to suspect how the matter lay. And
indeed he would have been glad enough to give
his consent to the marriage, had Rivalen but
spoken openly.

A little later, news came to Mark that an enemy had invaded his country in force. So Mark gathered together a goodly army and marched against the invader. In a great battle he vanquished him. Rivalen was foremost in the fight, striking and slaying like a valiant knight, but in the midst of the battle, he was stricken through the side with a spear, and carried half-dead from the field. With great sorrow they bore him home to Tintagel, and soon news came to Blancheflor, how that her lover was wounded near to death.

Great was the grief of Blancheflor! She durst confide it to no one, except to her faithful old nurse. Alone with this old woman, she stole from her lodging by night, and crept secretly and in disguise to where Rivalen lay, determined at least to see and kiss him once again before he should die.

She gave out that she was a wise woman come to heal Rivalen of his wound, and so came where he lay. And he, when he saw her, ordered his attendants to leave the chamber. So, coming to him, and seeing him pale and sick, she cried: "Ah! woe is me! Wherefore was I born? Farewell, all my joy and hope!"

Then she leaned over him and taking him in her arms, kissed and embraced him a thousand times, and he her again. Her lips breathed joy into his heart and strength into his body. In his sickness and his pain, he loved her and she yielded herself to him.

That night was conceived the child whose story you shall hear. Begotten in pain and conceived in sorrow, he lived to bring woe and grief on every man and woman that loved him.

Rivalen was tended by the most skilful leeches in the country, and in time he was healed of his wound. But no sooner was he recovered, than a messenger arrived in Cornwall, with the news that his enemy, Morgan, had invaded his territory with a mighty host. At once Rivalen let prepare a ship, and stored it well with horses and provender, and made ready for the voyage.

Woe now was Blancheflor! When Rivalen came to take his leave of her, she said to him: "Sweet love, what sorrow is now befallen me for the love of thee! Unless God help me, I am undone. Sorrow is mine, whether thou go or stay, for know, I am with child of thee. If thou go, I may have to suffer a shameful death. But it is better thou shouldst not stay, lest they slay thee too with me and make an orphan of our child, who otherwise may yet grow up to receive his due rank and honour at his father's hand."

So saying, she fainted in his arms. But when she was come to herself, Rivalen comforted her and set her at his side and said:

"Sweet love, I knew not this whereof thou now tellest me. Now will I do whatever shall seem best for thy honour. Either I will remain here with thee or thou shalt come home to my own

country with me. Choose thou; for as thou
shalt choose, so will I do."

So Blancheflor went home with Rivalen to
Armenye, where he found his people hard pressed
by Morgan. He summoned his faithful marshal,
Roald le Foytenant, by whose counsel he married
Blancheflor by rite of Church, but in private,
because the time was short. Then he left her in
the care of Roald in his castle of Kanoel and rode
forth with his men to encounter Morgan.

There were done many great feats of arms;
many shields broken; many brave men taken and
slain. There was Rivalen smitten through, so
that he fell dead from horse. His men brought
his body back to Kanoel.

When Blancheflor heard of it, she was so struck
with sorrow that she could not be comforted.
"Alas!" she cried, "how shall I live? He was
my joy and I his comfort. We should have died
together. Were I but delivered of this child, I
should go seek him in death."

Then she called Roald de Foytenant, and committed to his care the child that should be born
of her. She also gave him a ring which he might
show to King Mark, "for," said she, "when Mark
sees it, he will know that the child is his sister's."

Thereupon, she fell into the pains of labour.
At the end of three days and nights of bitter travail,
she gave birth to a son and died.

And they baptised the boy, and called him
Tristan, that is to say, "Triste homme." "Triste"

signifies " sad " and " homme " signifies " man " ;
therefore for the pains and sufferings of his parents,
he was called Tristan.   Rightly was he so named.
In sorrow was he conceived, in sorrow was he
born, sorrow was his portion by day and night,
sorrowfully he died.   Hearken and you shall hear.

CHAPTER TWO

HOW TRISTAN CAME TO CORNWALL

NOW Roald le Foytenant was afraid that if Duke Morgan learned there was a son born to Rivalen he would slay the child. So Roald gave out that his own wife was brought to bed of a boy, and brought Tristan up as his own son. He gave him a good master, who taught him the seven arts and the seven branches of music and to speak several languages. He learned also to ride and fence and fight as became a nobleman, and to hunt and chase, so that never was youth more skilled in venery. Moreover he was versed in all games that are played in kings' courts, and in the laws and customs of government. Each day he waxed in beauty and virtue, for he was richly gifted by nature.

When Tristan was about fourteen years old, it happened that a great merchant ship cast anchor on the shores of Armenye close by the castle. In it were merchants from Norway with a rich cargo of silks and jewels, furs, fish and beeves, oil and sulphur, and many noble falcons both grey and white. Tristan and his foster-brothers went down with Roald to visit the ship and buy such things as pleased them. Tristan, who knew many languages, was interpreter for the merchants.

Presently Tristan espied a chess-board and said to the merchants : " Which of you will play at chess with me ? " One of the Norwegians accepted his challenge and they sat down to play. Roald le Foytenant and his sons went home and left Tristan to his game. With him remained only the noble and courteous tutor who had brought him up. His name was Governal.

Now as Tristan played at chess, the Norwegians, seeing him so fair and skilled and learned, bethought them that he might be of great service to them. So they plotted to kidnap him, and while he was absorbed in the game, they softly cut the cables and slipped away to sea. The chess-board was set out beneath an awning that flapped and cracked noisily in the wind, so that neither Tristan nor Governal noticed that the ship was moving till they were already far from the land.

Then the treacherous sailors set Governal adrift upon the sea in a little rowing-boat, saying : " Go where thou wilt, sink or swim ; but the boy must come with us."

With great pains and hardship Governal made his way back to land, bringing the hard tidings that Tristan was carried off. He manned a ship and set forth in pursuit. He sailed first to Norway, then to Denmark, England, Ireland, the Orkneys

and Iceland, but nowhere could he find any trace
of Tristan.

Meanwhile Tristan, sorrowing and lamenting,
was carried in the merchantman almost to the
coasts of Norway. But a fearful tempest sprang
up and drove the ship hither and thither, and so
beat upon her that all feared she would founder.
Then the sailors cried out : " This is God's judg-
ment upon us for carrying away Tristan ! If He
will but bring us to land we swear to set the lad
free." Immediately the storm ceased and the sun
shone, and in a little time they came to land.

So they put Tristan ashore, and gave him food
and commended him to Heaven. Then they set
sail and departed.

Heavy at heart was Tristan thus left alone in an
unknown country. Whether it was Christian or
heathen he knew not. All about were rocks and
forests where wild beasts might be lurking. But
he considered that it was better to go forward
boldly than to perish where he stood. Accordingly, seeing several trodden paths, he chose one
of them, and presently it led him out of the forest.

Now Tristan was dressed in a rich surcoat and
mantle of silk, embroidered with fine gold and
furred with ermine. And as he went, he met
with two pilgrims returning from S. Michael's
Mount ; he saluted them courteously with this
greeting :

    " God's blessing on you, sirs," said he,
    " And on your holy company."

So they greeted him again and asked him whence he came and what he did in that place. Then said Tristan, " Sirs, I am a young nobleman of this country, and while hunting with my companions I have lost my way." (For he feared that if they knew him to be alone and friendless they might slay him for the sake of his rich dress.) " And you, sirs," said he, " whither go you ? " They said : " To Tintagel." " I also," said Tristan, " am going to Tintagel ; let us go together."

Now as they walked and talked together, they saw a hart come fleeing towards them, and after a great pack of hounds and brachets baying and pursuing. And presently the hart plunged into a stream and the hounds close upon him. And being hard pressed, he turned to bay then and there and was pulled down by the hounds, and the huntsmen coming up, cut his throat. After this, they were about to hew him in quarters like a stuck pig, but Tristan cried out :

" Stay ! What are you doing ? Whoever saw a hart hacked to pieces in that fashion ? Is that the custom of this country ? "

The chief huntsman replied courteously : " Such is indeed our custom, and we know no other. Knowest thou any other way ? "

" Yes, sir," said Tristan, " in my country we break up the hart in a seemly manner."

" Show us that," said the huntsman.

So Tristan showed them how to dismember the hart after the noble laws of venery—how to take off the shoulder, the haunch and the saddle, the fillets, the numbles and all the other parts, and to arrange the best portions on a stake, to be presented to the king. The huntsmen were filled with admiration and besought him to accompany them to the court. So Tristan went gladly with them. He told them that he was a rich merchant's son, who had left his home in order to see the world.

" What is your name, fair child ? "

" I am called Tristan," said he.

" Alas ! " said the chief huntsman, " could thy father find no happier name for thee, young sir so handsome and so gay ? "

As they were thus talking, they came within sight of the castle. " What kingly place is this ? " asked Tristan.

" Young sir, it is the Castle of Tintagel."

" Tintagel ! " cried Tristan, " blessed be thou and all that dwell within thee ! "

Then they sounded the horn before the gate and King Mark came forth to meet them. The huntsmen told Mark how they had met Tristan, and how he was a merchant's son of Armenye, and how he had taught them the right customs of the chase. Then said King Mark :

> " Tristan, Tristan of Armenye
> How courteous and how fair you be ! "

So the king graciously besought Tristan to stay at the court. He went hunting with the king and showed him how to dismember the deer. And when the harpers harped in hall, Tristan took the instrument and sang the lays of his own country— the song of Goron, the song of Graelent, the song of fair Thisbe the Babylonian. And so well did he harp and sing that they could never hear enough of his harping. And the king showed him great favour, and made him lie in his own chamber, and gave him a horse and put him in charge of his hawks and his armoury. And Tristan went everywhere with the king, and by night he lulled him to slumber with his harping.

Now leave we to speak of Tristan and speak we of Roald le Foytenant that sought him sorrowing in many countries. Great hardships he suffered by storm and tempest; his body was wasted with grief and toil. Three years he searched for him in vain, but at the beginning of the fourth year he came to Denmark, where whom should he meet but the two pilgrims who had been with Tristan when he met the huntsmen and had followed him to Tintagel. They told him how Tristan was living at the court in high favour with King Mark. Then was Roald glad. He sailed at once for Cornwall and made his way to the castle. He was well-nigh ashamed to present himself at the gate, for he was penniless and in rags after his long wanderings; nevertheless the porter received him courteously and led him into the hall, where Tristan was serving King Mark at table.

As soon as Tristan saw him, he ran to him and fell on his neck, and either made great joy of other.

D

Then Tristan took Roald by the hand and presented him to the king, who received him with all honour and let conduct him to a bath and clothe him in a rich dress and set him at the high table among the noblest of his lords.

Then Roald told the king the story of Tristan's birth—how he was in very deed the son of Mark's sister Blancheflor and of Rivalen, and in token of the truth he showed Mark the ring which Blancheflor had given him before she died. King Mark was greatly astonished to recognise his sister's ring, and before all the assembled knights and barons he received Tristan as his own dear nephew. All wept for tenderness to hear the pitiful tale of Tristan's parents and of the fidelity of Roald.

But Tristan fell at King Mark's feet and besought him to give him arms and dub him knight, which was done accordingly. And the king gave him rich arms and a tall destrier with red housings and gold lions embroidered thereon and a shield with the image of a wild boar. And he gave him twenty squires and a hundred knights to follow him.

With this force, Tristan returned to Brittany. And there he made war upon Duke Morgan and slew him and defeated his vassals in a great battle. Then he called all his own liegemen together and said : " Sirs, I am your own true liege, the son of Rivalen. But King Mark my uncle has no son nor heir but me. Therefore I will return to his court and serve him in all honour. But to my noble foster-father Roald I give this town and all my lands and to his heirs forever. I pray you, serve him faithfully."

Then he wept and embraced them all lovingly and after set sail for Cornwall. And they all lamented his going.

Thus Tristan avenged his parents upon Duke Morgan.

CHAPTER THREE

MORHOLT

WHEN Tristan returned to Cornwall, he
was greeted with sad news; the powerful Duke
Morholt had come from Ireland to claim tribute
from King Mark for the two countries which he
ruled, Cornwall and England.

Now this is what the true history tells us of the
origin of this tribute. It was first levied by
Gorman, King of Ireland, when King Mark was
but a youth. Gorman was more powerful than
Mark, and had become more formidable still
through his marriage to the sister of Morholt, for
Morholt was a great duke of Ireland, wealthy,
strong and holding wide fiefs.

And what was this tribute? I tell you no lie—
it was thus. The first year, three hundred pounds
of copper; the second year, the same of silver;
and the third year, of gold. And now Morholt
had come in force, ready armed for battle, to
collect the fourth year's tribute, and this time he
demanded three hundred of the noblest youths of
England and Cornwall.

The day that Tristan arrived in Cornwall was

the day when the nobles were to cast lots, which of their sons were to be taken. Great was the lamenting, piteous was the wailing of the mothers. But Morholt was so terrible a knight that none dared to refuse the tribute.

Tristan was indignant at this sight. He strode into the King's hall, and cried: "Noble lords, now may God save you and yours from shame and from dishonour! Is there not a man among you that will venture himself in combat against a single foe to rid you of this shameful tribute? If this be so, ye are serfs and no knights. Choose now a champion among you, strong and resolute, to withstand Morholt in single combat and send him home recreant to Ireland! If no better can be found, I am willing to set my life upon the hazard, for the love of my uncle the King. This man may be strong, but God is also strong to aid me. But rouse yourselves; quit this drawing of lots; Morholt will say that he has found none but cowards in this country!"

Then cried Mark: "Thanks, fair nephew! Come and embrace me. If thou canst win back our freedom for us, thou shalt be heir to all my kingdom."

So Tristan kissed his uncle and all the knights and nobles there present; and he gave the King his glove, in token that he was ready to do battle against Morholt. So Morholt was sent for, and he came into the hall, expecting to receive the tribute. But when he had sat down, Tristan strode up to him, crying:

"Lords! the King of Ireland demands tribute from you—not because it is just that you should pay, but because he in time past by force compelled it. But that which is taken by force is not held by right.

> "That which by force from us was ta'en
> We may by force take back again;
> Challenge for challenge, man for man,
> Now let him take the prize who can!"

Then said Morholt: "I hear your folly, and how you refuse to pay the tribute. Army against army, I cannot fight you, for I came hither with but a small force, not thinking to find you perjured. But choose you a man to fight against me in single combat. If any be so bold, there lies my glove!"

Then Tristan took up Morholt's gage of battle, saying: "I am he that will prove upon thy body that we are not perjured, nor ought we to pay tribute to Ireland."

So they fixed the third day thereafter for the combat.

And when the day came, Morholt armed himself. He rode a strong destrier, housed in steel, and he bore about his neck a huge and heavy shield, and in his hand a sharp, well-tempered sword.

Tristan also armed himself. He put on gambons of steel, with golden spurs upon his heels, and a strong hauberk, and about his waist King Mark girded a sword well-proved in many battles. On his head was a shining helm, about his neck a mighty shield, and they brought him a good brown horse, well harnessed for battle.

Now the place chosen for the combat was a little island in the sea, so close to the shore that the battle could be clearly seen from thence ; and it was agreed that none save the two champions should set foot upon the island so long as the fight lasted. Two boats lay upon the shore, one for each champion. Morholt first embarked, with his horse and his armour ; he took the oar, and rowed himself out to the island, and there he tied the boat to the shore, and mounted on his horse, and began to curvet and caracole upon the field of combat so beautifully that it was a pleasure to see him, and it seemed as though he had only come there to play and amuse himself.

Then Tristan in his turn embarked. All men trembled for him as he took leave of them, and prayed God to bless his arms. So Tristan pushed off the boat in the name of God. And when he reached the island, he let the boat drift away to seaward, and mounted at once upon his horse.

Then said Morholt : " What dost thou ? Wherefore dost thou let the boat drift away ? "

And Tristan said : " I will tell thee. Here are two men and only one boat. If we be not both slain, it is certain that one of us will soon lie dead upon this island. One boat is enough to carry the victor home."

Morholt was a strong and a tall knight, of great

valour, the wightest knight in Ireland. He covered himself with his shield, and couched his lance and spurred against Tristan. Tristan set lance in rest and rode against him. The shock of their meeting splintered the lances, but their strong shields guarded them from hurt. Then they drew their swords, and struck great blows, that the sparks flew from the swords and the helms and the hauberks. Tristan was valiant, but Morholt was strong and proved in many battles. Soon the helms were shattered, the hauberks smitten ring from ring, the shields cut in pieces and the ground strewn with iron and steel and the gold of their shields and crests. Long time the battle seemed doubtful.

Then in his rage, Tristan smote Morholt through the lifted shield and through the helm; he cleft the crest and shore away half the shield with its gems and gold; he burst the hauberk-rings and cut him open through flesh and bone and saddle-bow. A whole hand's-breadth did he plunge his sword into the body of the horse, and had the blade been longer it had gone farther still.

But as Tristan lifted his arm to smite, the sword of Morholt caught him upon the left breast, and bit through the mail and wounded him grievously upon the hip-bone.

Then said Morholt: "Better hadst thou done to pay the tribute, for thou art a dead man. My sword is poisoned, its wound is mortal. Never wilt thou find a leech to heal thy wound, save only my sister, Queen Iseult; she alone knows the secret of herbs and medicines for healing. Confess thyself vanquished; pay the tribute; henceforth we will be friends and companions, for never have I met a knight to equal thee."

Tristan replied: "Not for any offer thou canst make me shall my courage stoop; I would rather die upon the field than be dishonoured. God helping me, I will give thee blow for blow, and rid England of thee for ever. For all thou art triumphant now, this night shall see thy death."

Then, as Morholt set upon him again, Tristan lifted his sword with his whole strength and smote Morholt upon the helm; the iron bowed and the steel brake, the coif of mail split in twain and the sword cleft the brain-pan and remained fixed in the skull. Tristan sought to free it for another blow, but the blade broke and a piece of it was left in the bone. Morholt fell dead from his horse, and Tristan cried:

"Thy sister Iseult, indeed, may alone heal my wounds, but none shall ever heal thine. Whatever come of my hurt, thine is more grievous still!"

Then Tristan returned to shore in Morholt's boat. Great was the joy of the men of Cornwall, bitter was the grief of the Irish.

"Lords of Ireland," quoth Tristan, "get you home, and take with you your tribute that lies yonder on the island. And tell your master, next time he sends messengers for tribute to King Mark, we will send them back with the same honours as to-day ! "

So the Irishmen sailed away, taking the body of Morholt with them. And Tristan went back to the palace. And they sought physicians and drugs and ointments to heal his hurt, but all in vain, for his wound turned black, and his pain increased, and all feared that he must die of that venomed wound.

When the companions of Morholt brought the body home to Ireland, and gave the king Tristan's message, then was there great grief and mourning throughout the court.

And Queen Iseult came forth from his chamber with her daughter, Iseult the Fair. She wept, and lamented, and cursed England and the tribute of England and Tristan, who had slain her brother. And the men who stood by saw the piece of Tristan's sword sticking in Morholt's skull, and they drew it forth and gave it to Queen Iseult. So she washed away the brains and blood from it, and placed it in a casket, in memory of her loss. And they buried the body of Morholt with great honour.

CHAPTER FOUR

TANTRIS

NOW Tristan sought healing for his wound, but could find no leech in the kingdom that had skill to cure him. He was in such great pain that death seemed better than life. The poison burned him to the bone; his wound stank so that neither kindred nor friend could come near him.

At length Tristan said to the king:

"Sir, I pray thee, let me go far away, and wander at God's will, and take what He shall send. For here I cannot stay."

And the king replied:

"Alas, fair nephew! wilt thou seek thy death? Nay then, if thou must go, then will I give thee a ship, well furnished with all things needful."

So Tristan thanked Mark, and the ship was made ready. And Governal said that he would follow Tristan, whether it were for death or for healing. So Tristan set sail and Governal with him, and of all his other possessions he took with him nothing, save only his harp.

And they let the ship drive before the wind, as God should direct it. Many days were they tossed

upon the ocean, not knowing whither they went,
but at length they saw land before them, and
presently a harbour, out of which a boat came
towards them and hailed them. And when they
asked the name of that land, they were told:

"This land is Ireland, and this port is Dublin."
Now when Tristan learned whither the winds
had brought him, he trembled lest the King of
Ireland should learn who he was. Therefore he
bethought him to turn his name about, and when
they asked him who he was, he said:

"I am called Tantris. I was bound for Spain
in a merchantman, when pirates robbed the vessel
and killed the crew and sorely wounded me."

So the Irish sailors brought Tantris back with
them to the harbour; and all day he charmed
them by his playing of the harp and by his courtly
accomplishments. At length the news of this
came to the palace, and when Princess Iseult the
Fair heard of it, she besought her father and mother
to let Tristan come and teach her how to play the
harp, and write, and compose songs and music.

So Tristan was brought into the queen's chamber.
But when Queen Iseult saw how evilly wounded
he was, and how no one could come nigh him
for the stinking of his sore, she had pity on him
and said:

"I will heal thee, Tantris, for my daughter
Iseult's sake, that thou mayest thereafter be her
tutor in all courtly learning."

Then she bade them place a certain plaster on

the wound and leave it till nightfall. And when it had drawn away all the evil odour, she with her own hand dressed the wound with herbs and drugs of wondrous power, so as quickly to reduce the swelling and inflammation. She cut away the dead flesh and charmed away the poison which remained in the wound, and dressed the place with ointments so skilfully that in forty days Tantris was whole and sound once more, and had recovered all his former beauty. For she knew every secret of herbs and medicines ; she knew the antidotes to all poisonous draughts and poisoned weapons ; there was no physician on earth so cunning as she.

When Tantris was whole again, he set himself to teach the young Iseult how to play the harp and to write and to sing, and she was so apt a pupil that soon the fame of her learning went throughout the country.

The king and queen of Ireland were well pleased. But Tristan feared all the time lest he should be discovered. Therefore, as soon as he had quite recovered his strength, he went to the queen and besought her to give him his ship again and let him return to his own country.

"For," said he, "Lady, I thank you for your kindness towards me. For all that you have done for me, I will ever be your loving servitor. Yet I would fain see my friends again, who know not where I am, nor whether I be alive or dead."

And the queen grieved to lose Tantris. But she gave him her leave to go, and let make ready his ship with all things needful for the voyage, and gave him a mark of pure gold at parting. Tristan thanked her for her kindness and for her rich presents, and bade her farewell.   He took his harp in hand and harped a tune ; and so set sail from Ireland with a favourable wind.

CHAPTER FIVE

THE FIGHT WITH THE DRAGON
AND THE WOOING OF ISEULT

WHEN Tristan returned whole and sound to Cornwall, King Mark welcomed him with joy, and listened eagerly while he told how the Queen of Ireland had healed him with her magic skill and how the fair Princess Iseult excelled all women in the world for beauty and praise. But the nobles in their hearts were jealous of Tristan; they envied his valour, craft and beauty; and they feared lest he should become king over them at Mark's death.

Accordingly they took counsel together and came to Mark, saying:

" Sire, it behoves you to marry a wife, who may give you a lawful heir. Otherwise, if you should die, your realm will be exposed to strife and usurpation. Know, therefore, that we will serve you no longer, save you marry a wife."

King Mark replied: " Thanks, lords; but God has already given us an heir to the throne. Tristan is my heir; while he lives, wife nor queen shall never sit by my side."

Then the hatred of the nobles waxed hot against Tristan, so that he besought Mark, for both their sakes, to yield to the will of the barons.

So Mark called the barons together and told them that he would consent to what they wished; only they must choose him a wife, fair, noble, courteous, equal to him by birth, beauty and breeding (for he thought in this manner to put obstacles in the way of the marriage).

But one of the barons thought of a plot to destroy Tristan by means of this matter, and so said to the king:

" Such a maiden is easily found. You have heard Tristan's report of the beauty, courtesy and wisdom of Iseult, the king's daughter of Ireland. If you will not have her, then we shall know that you are determined to have no wife at all, for Tristan has testified that she is worthy in every way to be your choice."

The king replied: " That is true; but how can I think to wed Iseult? Her father Gorman and I have been deadly enemies these many years."

Then answered the wily barons: " Sire, send Tristan to fetch Iseult. He knows the language and the country; he sits high in favour with Iseult and her mother; who so fit as he to win the maiden for you, either by force, by cunning or by persuasion? "

Then Tristan saw full well that he was taken in a trap; but since there was no help, he stood forth and said:

" Sire, true it is that I know the country and the king of Ireland, and the queen and her daughter Iseult ; but true it is also that I slew the queen's brother Morholt ; and if I go again to win Iseult for you, and the king learns who I am, I shall not escape with my life. Nevertheless, I will go, and if I come not again with Iseult, never will I set foot in this country more."

So Tristan prepared a fine ship, well stored with gold and raiment and wine and rich provisions, and set sail for Ireland. And learning that Gorman held his court at Wexford, he landed there, and presented himself to the king in the guise of a merchant, who sought permission to trade. This was granted, and the ship anchored in the port of Wexford. But the Cornishmen did no trade that day, but sat playing chess and draughts and making good cheer among the men of Ireland.

Next day they were awakened by a terrible clamour in the town, and saw all the people running hither and thither, and fleeing in great disorder towards the sea. This alarm was caused by a fierce dragon, which lived in those parts, and every day came down into the town, spewing out flames and devouring all that came in its way. King Gorman had made proclamation that whoever was brave enough to slay the dragon should have his daughter's hand in marriage. Many had tried to do so, but all so far had perished in the attempt.

When Tristan heard this, he inquired where

the dragon's lair might be, and at what hour it was accustomed to sally out and trouble the town. Saying nothing to anyone, he waited till nightfall ; then took his horse and arms and went to lie in wait.

At the first gleam of daybreak, the dragon came out, as it was wont, and made towards Wexford. Tristan heard its horrible cry and rode to meet it. On the way he met a troop of armed knights, fleeing in terror from its approach, but he disregarded their warnings and rode on.

Then close before him he saw the dragon ; its hideous head towering, its eyes gleaming, its open jaws spitting fire and poison all about it. Horribly roaring, the dragon leapt upon Tristan, but Tristan spurred his horse and struck the monster so fiercely upon the head that his lance smashed the great teeth in its mouth, smote through its neck and plunged deep into its body. His horse fell dead in the sheets of flame which gushed from the dragon's throat, but he leapt lightly from it and advanced, sword in hand. Long time did Tristan fight the dragon, till his head was giddy and his armour burnt black with fire, but at last his sword found the heart of the brute, and the dragon fell down dead.

Then Tristan cut off the dragon's tongue at the root and put it in his bosom, and went quietly aside to a stream, to wash and refresh himself. But the heat of his body drew out the poison

from the dragon's venomed tongue. It penetrated
his breast and overcame him, so that he fell down,
speechless, helpless, black and swollen, by the
water-side.

Now there was a certain seneschal, a false and
cowardly man, who had long wished to wed the
Princess Iseult, but though each day he had put
on his armour and gone out against the dragon,
he had always been afraid to face it when he saw
it. Indeed, he was one of the men whom Tristan
had met fleeing that morning, and he had waited
in hiding till the sudden silence told him that the
dragon was dead. When all was safe, he ventured
to the spot, and seeing the dead body of the dragon,
but no Tristan, he supposed that before dying
the monster had killed and eaten the brave
knight.

The seneschal hastily cut off the head of the
dragon and rode a-gallop back to the town, crying :
" I have killed the dragon ! I have killed the
dragon ! Now, King, perform thy promise and
give me thy daughter Iseult ! "

When the king heard this, he knew he must
keep his word, and appointed the next day to
give Iseult to the seneschal. But the princess
wept and lamented, for she hated the false seneschal ; and she said to her mother :

" Never will I consent to be this man's wife !
I will kill myself rather. But I cannot believe
that such a coward as he ever slew the terrible
dragon. Let us go and look where the monster's

body lies. It may be we shall find there the true hero, whether living or dead I know not."

So the two ladies went forth to the place where the dragon lay, and there they saw Tristan's horse, burnt and blackened with fire.

Then said Iseult : " This horse never belonged to the seneschal, but to the true slayer of the dragon. Let us seek further."

Next they saw the shield of Tristan, gleaming with gold and painted with his cognisance.

Then said Iseult : " This shield was never the seneschal's. It is gilded within and without, and not of the fashion of our country. But what is become of the true dragon-slayer ? "

Then they went further and found Tristan lying senseless beside the stream. They saw at once that he was poisoned, but not dead, and soon by her skill and her healing medicines the queen brought him back to life. Then she had him conveyed by stealth to her own apartments, and there she anointed his wounds and gave him remedies against the poison, while the Princess waited tenderly upon him.

Next day the seneschal came to the palace with the dragon's head in his hand, to claim the hand of Iseult. King Gorman assured him that he would duly pay the reward, and sent two knights to call the queen and the Fair Iseult into the hall.

But meanwhile, Tristan was fully recovered, and the queen said to him :

" Friend, who art thou ? Whence art thou ?

How didst thou kill the dragon ? Strangely dost thou resemble Tantris that was here not long ago."

Tristan answered : " Yes, I am Tantris. I came hither with my friends, who are merchantmen. And when I knew of the dragon, I set forth as beseems a knight and slew it and cut out its tongue and put it in my bosom ; but the poison overcame me and I fell down lifeless ; and of the rest I know nothing, save that you have rescued me, and for that I will serve you all the days of my life."

Then the queen told him of the seneschal's treachery. And Tristan answered :

" I will prove that the seneschal did not slay the dragon ; and I will defend Iseult from him with my body."

Then Tristan sent down to the ship for Governal, and his other companions. And they brought with them fine raiment and put it upon him, so that no king's son could have been more richly arrayed. And when the time was come, they went with Tristan and the queen and the Fair Iseult into the hall to confront the seneschal. And the Irish wondered to see the beauty of Tristan and his companions.

Then the seneschal demanded the hand of Iseult in marriage as his reward for slaying the dragon. But Iseult laughed him to scorn, saying :

" Thou ? thou the dragon-slayer ? Thou that wast ever known to be cowardly, false, a traitor in grain? Not so; for they say that another slew the dragon, and thou wouldst steal the reward."

The seneschal answered: "Who tells this lie of me? Show him to me, and I will prove it upon his body!"

Then Tristan stepped forward and said:

"Here am I. I slew the dragon, and I will do battle against you in proof thereof, whensoever the king shall determine."

So they exchanged their gages of battle, and the king appointed a day to decide the cause between them. And he made the queen answerable upon her life that Tristan would appear at the appointed time.

Now it chanced one day, when Tristan was in his bath, and the Princess Iseult was attending upon him, that she began idly to examine his armour and weapons that he had laid aside.

"Ah!" thought she, "here is the helm— proud is the head it covers; here is the breast-plate, and valiant is the heart it defends; here is a mighty sword indeed, and held in a strong hand; a fit weapon to defend a man's life and deal death to his enemies, if so be the dragon's poisonous breath have not harmed the steel."

So she drew the sword from the scabbard, and there beheld the notch that was made in the blade the day Tristan slew Morholt. She wondered how that notch had come there, for it seemed to her an older matter than the fight with the dragon. And as she looked, she remembered.   She went to the casket in which she kept the fragment of steel which she had taken from Morholt's head.   And when she set the fragment to the blade, they fitted perfectly together.

Then fury filled her, and she ran upon Tristan with the sword, crying :

" Villain and traitor, thou canst not now deceive me !   Die upon the sword with which thou didst slay my uncle !"

Then cried Tristan : " Stay !   Hear me first, then do as thou wilt.   Twice hast thou saved my life : once from the poison of the venomed sword, when I taught thee to sing and play upon the harp ; and once again, when thou foundest me stretched by the water-side.   Slay me now if thou wilt, helpless, in my bath—if thou didst save me only to slay me.   Slay me—but remember that I am pledged to do battle with the seneschal, and that thy mother is answerable with her life for my appearance."

Then Iseult bethought her that her only choice lay between Tristan and the evil seneschal, and she let the sword's point fall.   She wept for her fate, and as she thought of the wrong that Tristan had done her, she grasped the hilt again ; but when she thought of the seneschal, the wrath went out of her.

When the queen came in and heard who Tristan was, she claimed the right to slay him herself, in vengeance for her brother ; but Iseult held her back, reminding her of the word she had pledged to the king. So each of the two women restrained the other. And Tristan knelt at their feet, saying:

"Queen, have pity! For thine own honour came I to Ireland. For, ever since that first voyage when I came to thee for healing, I have not ceased to proclaim to King Mark, my liege lord, the praise of thee and of thy daughter Iseult. Now therefore hath he sent hither by me to ask thy daughter's hand in marriage, and for this cause did I slay the dragon, that the Lady Iseult might be queen and mistress of the realm of England and Cornwall."

When they heard this, the ladies sent to call the king, and when he had come they fell at his feet, saying:

"Sire, grant us a boon."

"Willingly," said Gorman, "so it be not contrary to right and justice."

Then said the queen: "This man is Tristan, the slayer of my brother. Nevertheless, since he has killed the dragon, I beseech you to pardon him the death of Morholt on condition that he will rid us of the claims of the false seneschal."

"Very well," said the king; "seeing that I have promised to grant your boon; seeing moreover that you, who are the persons most injured by the death of Morholt, are ready to forgive him, I will do as you desire."

Then Tristan thanked the king, and said:

"Hearken, sire. The great and puissant King Mark of England sends you this message. He prays you to give him the hand of your daughter Iseult in marriage. He will bestow all Cornwall upon her as her dowry, and she shall reign with him over all England; and there shall be peace and good-will between England and Ireland."

The king replied : " So be it, upon mine honour ! Swear now to me that there shall be no treachery upon your part, and I will send my daughter Iseult home with you to King Mark."

So they let bring in the Holy Relics, and Tristan made oath for Mark that he would be faithful to this covenant.

Now when the day came for Tristan to meet the seneschal, King Gorman called all his barons together and led Tristan into the hall, and said :

" Bear witness, lords, that I have duly stood bail for Tristan, and produced him at the time appointed. Now let the seneschal stand forth."

So the seneschal made his claim, saying :

" Sire, I demand the hand of the Princess Iseult in marriage, according to thy promise, for I have slain the dragon, and here is its head in proof of my story."

Then said Tristan :

" Liar and villain ! Here is the dragon's head indeed, but where is its tongue ? Look, lords, and see for yourselves. I myself slew the dragon, and I have the tongue here in my hand. Let this boaster admit that he lies—else let him stand to his weapons, for I will prove it upon him in single combat !"

And when the barons saw the tongue and how that it fitted the throat of the dragon, they fell to mocking and deriding the false boastful seneschal, so that he fled away; and thereafter he was held in scorn for ever by all noble men.

CHAPTER SIX

THE PHILTRE

AFTER this, King Mark called the barons of Ireland together, and told them of Tristan's embassy and how he had promised his daughter's hand to King Mark of England. All agreed that this alliance was an honourable one and favourable to both parties, since it gave assurance of a lasting peace between Ireland and Britain.

So they made great preparations for the departure of Iseult, that they might speed her with all honour and magnificence upon her wedding journey as became a great king's daughter.

But the queen her mother brewed by her magic art a wondrous philtre of many strange flowers and herbs. She made it such that no living man and woman might drink thereof together but they should love one another with an enduring love, until their lives should end. And she poured the philtre into a little flacket, and gave it to a young maid called Brangwain, that was to accompany Iseult to Cornwall.

"Brangwain," said the queen, "take great care of this little flask. The first night, when Iseult

and King Mark are abed together and Mark calls
for wine, give this drink to both of them at once.
Beware that none drink of it save they two only.
Set not thy lips to it.   It is a love-potion."

Brangwain replied : " Madam, it shall be done
as thou commandest."

So, when all things were in readiness, they went
down to the shore together at the flood-tide, the
king and queen accompanying Iseult.   And the
men and women of the country wept to see Iseult
depart, for they all loved her dearly because of her
beauty and courtesy.   As soon as Iseult had embarked, the sailors hoisted the sails, and the ship
sped on her way with a favouring wind.   And
Iseult wept at thus leaving her home and her
parents and her friends for a land of strangers.
Sighing, she cried : " Would that I had died
before I came hither ! "   And Tristan comforted
her with kind words as best he might.

Now as they sailed the sun shone and the
weather was hot and oppressive.   Tristan therefore grew thirsty and called for wine.   One of his
pages ran to fetch it, and by ill-hap his eye lit upon
the flask that the queen had given to Brangwain,
and he poured the drink into a goblet and brought
it to Tristan.   And Tristan pledged Iseult in the
goblet, drinking half himself and giving the rest
to her.   Thus were they betrayed by that subtle
potion ; thus did the error of a little page doom
them to a life of sorrows and griefs, of endless
torments and joys unspeakable.

But when Brangwain saw what had happened, she stood aghast. "Alas, Tristan!" she cried, "Alas, Iseult! this potion is your death!"

Now as the philtre began to work, Tristan and Iseult began to look strangely upon one another. The sweet poison of love moved in their veins and tormented them, so that their tongues stammered and words came brokenly. Iseult moved restlessly as though in pain. At length Tristan said in a low voice:

"Tell me, fair lady, what is it troubles thee?"

Iseult replied in the Breton language:

"*L'amer* torments me; *l'amer* lies heavy on my heart; *l'amer* is pain and grief to me."

And Tristan knew not what to think, for in the Breton tongue the words *l'amer* have three meanings. There is *l'amer*, bitterness; there is *la mer*, the sea; and there is *l'amer*, which means love. Of these three meanings, there was one which he dared not think of; he set aside Love, their common lord and master, their mutual comfort and desire, and spoke only of the other two.

"Fair Iseult," said he, "thou wouldst say that the sea and its bitterness torment thee. Thou dost feel the salt taste of the sea and the bitterness of the wind."

"No, no, fair sir, not so; I do not feel either wind or sea. *L'amer* alone torments me."

Then Tristan knew that this riddle had but one meaning, and whispered softly:

"I also, fairest and dearest; Love and thou—these are my torment also."

And from that moment the heart of Tristan was wholly given to Iseult, and Iseult gave herself wholly to Tristan, with such utter love that nothing thenceforth could separate them for ever.

And all this time the ship sped under full sail towards England.

CHAPTER SEVEN

BRANGWAIN

NOW as they drew near the land of Cornwall, Iseult was seized with fear lest Mark should discover that she had given her maidenhead to Tristan. She therefore persuaded Brangwain to take her place in Mark's bed upon the bridal night; and Brangwain consented, knowing that her own carelessness had been the cause of the fatal love-draught.

So Iseult landed in Cornwall and was married to Mark with great pomp and rejoicing. And when they were got to bed, Tristan put out the lights and Brangwain took Iseult's place and thus Mark lay with her. And Thomas relates that when Mark had fallen asleep, Iseult came to bed, and Brangwain afterwards gave King Mark all that remained of the love-potion. But Iseult would not drink of it again. And Mark loved Iseult all his life thereafter.

Thus Iseult lived in great honour as Mark's wife and queen, and Tristan was placed in attendance on her, and they often met and loved in secret.

But after a time, Iseult began to fear lest Brangwain might betray the secret of her love for Tristan. Then, in her terror, she sent for two serfs, and bade them take Brangwain into the forest and slay her.

"Dear friend," said she to Brangwain, "I am sick. Go therefore into the forest and seek healing herbs for me; these men will escort thee and bring thee safely back."

Brangwain went willingly; but when they were at a good distance from the castle one of the serfs drew his sword and told her that she must prepare to die by the queen's command.

Then Brangwain said, weeping: "Be it so; but hear me before I die, and take this message to the queen. Tell her, I never did her wrong but once. When we sailed from Ireland, each of us had a smock white as snow. I kept mine clean and spotless; but Iseult wore hers night and day till it was soiled, and not fit for her to wear on her wedding night. In this necessity, I lent her mine; it may be that the garment displeased her, and for this cause she seeks to kill me. But save this fault, I know none. Greet her, therefore, from me; say that I thank her for her past kindness and forgive her my death. And now, strike when thou wilt!"

The serfs were touched by Brangwain's distress, so they tied her then and there to a tree and returned to the castle and told Iseult how that Brangwain was dead, and with what words she died. Then Iseult was seized with remorse and cried :

" Wretched slaves ! how dared you slay my servant ! You shall answer for her death ! I will have you torn in pieces if you cannot bring back Brangwain safe and sound."

Overjoyed, the serfs ran to the forest and released Brangwain and brought her back to the castle. Then Iseult fell upon her neck and kissed her and they were reconciled together. And Brangwain acted as go-between for Iseult and Tristan ; for such was the power of the love-potion that these twain might not live apart from one another ; for whenever they were separated they fell into grief and sickness.

CHAPTER EIGHT

PLOT AND COUNTER-PLOT

ONE day when Tristan was away hunting there came a tall ship to Cornwall, bearing a proud and valiant baron of Ireland. He came to the court, carrying neither sword nor lance, but only a harp of gold. Iseult recognised him, for he was one that had long loved her, and King Mark received him kindly for her sake.

After supper, the barons began to make mock of him for thus carrying his harp about him, but Mark courteously desired him to sing to them a song of Ireland. And he promised him in guerdon whatsoever gift he would.

So the harper sang two songs, so sweetly that it was a joy to hear him. And when he had finished :

" King," said he, " now grant me my promised reward."

" Willingly," said Mark, " say on ; what wouldst thou ? "

Then said the harper :

" Give me Iseult, for I desire her and her only, of all the treasures in thy kingdom."

"Nay," said Mark, "that will I never!"

"Then," said the other, "I call all thy barons to witness that thou art perjured. And if any will deny it, let him try out the cause with me in single combat."

But there was no Cornish baron that would do battle with the Irishman. So Mark was forced to keep his word, and he delivered over Iseult to the harper, who took her down to the sea-shore and set her in his pavilion. And Iseult wept, saying: "If Tristan had been here, he would have fought for me."

Now the Irish lord could not set sail at once, for the tide was out and the vessel lay high and dry. Meanwhile, Tristan returned from hunting. When he heard what had happened he took a fiddle in his hand and went down to the shore. There he found the harper seeking to comfort the weeping Iseult.

"Sir," said Tristan, "they tell me you are going to Ireland. I too am of that country; I pray you let me go with you."

"Nay, fellow," said the Irishman, "but if thou canst by thy fiddling restore the spirits of my lady-love, then will I give thee a cloak and a rich gown."

"That can I," said Tristan. "When she has heard me play her heart will never know sorrow."

So he played and sang a beautiful song, and Iseult's heart was gladdened by the sweet sound and by the love of her friend.

Then said one of the Irishmen to his lord :

" Sir, make haste. The tide is risen ; the ship is afloat ; better depart, lest Tristan return and find you here."

The baron replied : " What care I for Tristan ! Fiddler, play on ; sing us the lay of *Dido Queen of Carthage*."

So Tristan played on, and they all sat ravished by his melody, till now the sea was risen so far that it covered the gangway to the ship.

" What is to be done now ? " said the Irish baron. " How can my lady-love go aboard ? "

Tristan replied : " I have a good horse hard by. I will fetch him, and carry her over dry-shod."

So Tristan fetched his horse and took Iseult up behind him. Then he drew his sword and cried :

" Fool ! What was won by the harp is lost by the fiddle. You took Iseult by a trick ; and I have taken her back by guile."

So he spurred his horse and carried away his lady to the forest, where they passed the night joyously together. And in the morning he took her home to Mark, and warned him, saying :

" By my faith, sire, a woman is hard put to it to love a man who can give her away for a tune."

.   .   .   .   .   .

Before long it began to be whispered about the court that Tristan and the queen were too familiar ; but all was mere suspicion without proof.

Now Tristan lodged in the same chamber with a knight of the court named Mariadoc. One night, when Mariadoc was asleep, Tristan rose and stole out to the orchard, where there was a broken palisade by which he was accustomed to creep in secretly. Here Brangwain met him and brought him in to the queen; but by some mischance, as she went out, she left the chamber-door ajar.

Meanwhile, Mariadoc dreamed a fearful dream of a wild boar which sprang upon Mark's bed and gored the king with its tusks and befouled the bed with blood and slaver.

He woke in alarm and called to Tristan, but got no answer, and searching about, found his place empty and the door open. Wondering, he went out. It was bright moonlight and snow had fallen; he saw the tracks of Tristan's feet leading to the orchard, and following them, came to the broken palisade. He knew not what to think, but supposed that Tristan had gone to visit one of the queen's waiting-women. So, still following the footmarks, he came to the palace. All was still; a faint light glimmered through an open door; and looking in, he saw Tristan and the queen together.

This treachery filled him with wrath, hatred and envy. He went softly away, as though he had seen nothing, and said no word of the matter to Tristan when he returned. But the next day he took Mark aside and warned him of what was being said about Tristan and Iseult. The simple and loving heart of Mark was astonished; very unwilling was he to hear one word against Iseult whom he loved so dearly; and Mariadoc would not tell him that he himself had seen clear proof of her guilt, for he feared the vengeance of Tristan.

At length King Mark resolved to put Iseult to the test. He told her that he was going away on pilgrimage, and asked who she thought was the best person to take care of her in his absence.

Iseult said:

"Nay, my dear lord, who but Tristan, your own sister's son and the best man in your realm?"

The king reported this answer to Mariadoc, who said: "Why, here is proof enough how well she loves him." But Mark still hesitated.

But when Iseult told Brangwain of this conversation, and rejoiced at the thought of the happy hours she would be able to spend with Tristan, Brangwain saw through the plot, and said:

"This is only a trick of Mariadoc's to make you betray yourself. I have heard how he puts rumours about and whispers in the king's ear. Listen; next time the king speaks of this matter, you must say thus and thus."

The next night, therefore, when the king spoke further about his journey, and of leaving Iseult in Tristan's care, the queen said to him:

"Alas, sire, are you in earnest? I thought you but spoke in jest to tease me! Do you then love me so little, that you will leave me so soon?

Alone, in a strange land, far from my own people, who shall succour and comfort me?"

"Who but Tristan?" said Mark, astonished.

"Tristan?" said Iseult. "Tristan is no true friend to me. He pretends to love and serve me with flattering words, but that is only because he fears lest I take vengeance for the murder of my uncle. I have done what I could to seem friendly to him—for I know women are often reproached with disliking their husbands' kindred—but in very truth I detest him and would that I might never see him again."

And Mark believed her. But when he told this to Mariadoc, the latter said: "This is more deceit. I will teach you how to test her honesty."

So the next night, Mark said to Iseult:

"My journey is all arranged, and go I must. But since you so dislike my nephew Tristan, I will send him back to Armenye."

"Do not do that," said Iseult. "It will be said everywhere that you sent him away because I hated him, and envied him his inheritance. This will cause strife between you and your kindred on my account. Moreover, he is the strongest knight in your realm. If war should break out I should not know how to defend myself, and everyone would say that it was my fault that Tristan was sent away."

These words filled the king with grief and suspicion. In the morning, when Iseult told Brangwain what had passed, Brangwain blamed her folly and told her what she ought now to say to the king to allay his doubts.

So the next night, Iseult said to Mark :

" Were you indeed serious when you promised to send Tristan away ? Were I sure of this, how glad I should be ! How great would be this proof of your love to me. And I have thought : if any harm should happen to you upon your journey, Tristan would immediately take the opportunity to dishonour me and seize your kingdom for himself. Now, therefore, either send him home, or take him with you and leave me in the care of Mariadoc. Or, if you will, let me accompany you on your journey. I pray you, do what you will with me in all things, for if only I may please you, I care nothing for kindred or country or anything in comparison with your pleasure."

Thus she flattered Mark, and he believed her and held Mariadoc for a liar ; who yet had told him nothing but the truth.

CHAPTER NINE

THE DWARF

MARIADOC now tried another plan to open the king's eyes. He took into his counsel a certain sly and cunning dwarf, who was not only a favourite with Mark but also was allowed to go familiarly about in the women's apartments. The dwarf kept watch upon the lovers, and soon made such report of them to Mark that he determined to banish Tristan from the court.

So Tristan went to lodge in the town without the castle walls, and saw Iseult no more. And the lovers became sick and pale with grievous longing, so that the whole court remarked it, and so did the king. Therefore, to see what they would do, Mark called his huntsmen together and made believe to depart for a long hunting expedition in the forest. Tristan excused himself from accompanying the king, on the plea of sickness.

Now Brangwain thought of a plan to bring the lovers together. She went secretly to Tristan and said :

" You know the stream that runs from the spring in the orchard and flows beneath Iseult's chamber-window? Come down to the orchard; cut chips of wood from the trees; mark them with a T and an I and float them down the stream. When Iseult sees them, she will come and join you in the orchard."

Tristan carried out this plan, and the lovers met in safety many times. But one day the dwarf spied him throwing the chips into the stream and saw how, soon after, the queen came to him.

Next day he came to Tristan's lodging and found him cutting chips of wood from a branch. And the dwarf said to Tristan:

"The queen desires earnestly to see you to-night. She begs you not to fail her. Give me your answer quickly, for I must not stay too long, lest any should suspect me of being the messenger between you."

Tristan replied warily:

"I thank thee for thy message. Greet Queen Iseult from me, but say that I am sick, and cannot by any means attend upon her this evening. To-morrow I will come without fail. In the meanwhile I give thee this ermine cloak for thy pains."

But the dwarf had seen what Tristan was doing, and knew that he was preparing to meet the queen that night. So he went to the king's hiding-place and told him that if he would keep watch by the spring that night he should see Iseult meet her lover. Then Mark came secretly to the orchard and climbed into a pine-tree that stood beside the spring; and presently Tristan came, threw the chips into the stream and sat down beneath the tree to wait for Iseult.

Now every evening Iseult was wont to watch the stream for a message from Tristan. When she saw the chips floating, she wrapped herself in a mantle of ermine and hastened to the trysting-place beneath the tree where Mark sat watching.

But presently, as the moon rose and flooded the orchard with light, Tristan saw the shadow of King Mark reflected in the stream. He trembled, fearing that Iseult might not see it and so might betray herself. But she, coming, beheld the shadow also, and said immediately to Tristan:

"I am greatly astonished, Sir Tristan, that you should have asked me to meet you in such a place and at such an untimely hour. Think, if this were known, what colour it would give to the unjust suspicions men have of us! How unjust they are, you know well, for I swear to God that never have I shown love or desired to show love to any man, save only to him who first held me, maiden, within his arms!"

Tristan replied: "Madam, I know too well what vexations you have suffered on my account. I have made up my mind to quit the country, and am come hither to beg you to make my peace with the king and pray him that he will pay me my wage and give me leave to go."

So they parted; and Mark repented him that ever he had doubted these two whom he loved so well. He swore vengeance upon their traducers, recalled Tristan to the court, and restored both wife and nephew to his full grace and favour.

But Mariadoc bided his time.

One day, it chanced that King Mark had sent for the surgeon to bleed him, and both Iseult and Tristan were let blood also. And at night there were in the king's chamber only Iseult, Tristan, Brangwain and the evil dwarf, who had contrived a fresh plot to entrap the lovers.

Then Mark, counselled by the dwarf, bade Tristan put out all the lights. And when it was dark, the dwarf rose secretly and strewed flour upon the floor between Tristan's bed and the queen's. But the watchful Brangwain saw him, and warned Tristan.

In the middle of the night, the king rose, and called the dwarf to follow him, saying that he was going to hear mattins. Then Tristan wondered how he might come to Iseult without leaving footmarks in the flour; and standing upon the edge of his bed he leapt with both feet together into the queen's bed. But with the exertion, the vein that had been bled opened again, and drenched the bed with blood. And when he had taken his pleasure with Iseult, Tristan leaped back into his own bed again.

When morning was come, the king returned. He looked at the floor, and saw no footmarks in the flour. But he saw the bed of Iseult stained with blood. He asked her how this was, and

Iseult answered that her arm had bled where she had been let blood.

Then the king looked at Tristan's bed, and saw that it also was bloody, and his heart was filled with grief, for he knew that Iseult had lied to him.

CHAPTER TEN

THE ORDEAL BY FIRE

In his distress, Mark sought counsel of his ablest counsellors; for this matter touched his honour and the safety of his realm.

Some said on this manner and some on that, but at length a wise and aged bishop spoke as follows:

"Sire, you cannot as yet proceed publicly against the queen, for you have no direct and certain proof of her guilt. The queen is your lawful wife before God, and you must not repudiate her upon a mere suspicion. But let her be summoned to appear before us now; we will tell her of the accusation brought against her, and we will hear what answer she can make."

Iseult was accordingly bidden to appear before the court and the Bishop informed her of the charge, and called upon her to refute it.

The queen replied: "My lords, I am not ignorant of the rumours that are put about by my enemies. Alas! it is easy for them to cast suspicion upon a lonely woman in a strange land. But I am ready to face any trial. I beseech the king to let me prove my innocence by the ordeal of the red-hot iron. If I fail therein, I will be burned at the stake or torn to pieces by wild horses!"

The king agreed to this, and appointed the trial to be held at Carlion one month from then.

Now Iseult arranged with Tristan what he should do to save her. She told him that she would cross the river by boat at Carlion; he was to disguise himself and go down to the landing-place, and was to see to it that he was ready at hand to carry her from the boat to the shore. She would then tell him what to do.

So Tristan put on a peasant's dress, and stained his face brown, and wrapped himself about in an old cloak, and took his place at the time appointed. And when the ferry-boat came over with the queen aboard, she made a sign to Tristan and called out:

"Hither, thou! thou seemest a stout fellow. Come and carry me to land."

Tristan waded in and took Iseult up in his arms. And as he was carrying her, she whispered to him:

"Let thyself fall when we reach the shore."

So as they were mounting the river-bank, Tristan stumbled and fell. And the queen's garments being lifted about her to keep them from the water, he fell and lay between her naked thighs.

The queen's servants rushed forward in anger to beat Tristan, but she laughed and said:

"Spare the poor fellow. He is a pilgrim come

from a far country. His long travels have made him weak."

So, laughing at the clumsy pilgrim, they came to Carlion. There the iron was heated red-hot and blessed by three bishops. And there Iseult heard Mass and distributed generous alms to the people.

Then Iseult came forward, bare-foot, and clothed in sackcloth, so that all men wept at the pitiful sight. And she stretched forth her hand upon the Holy Relics and said :

" King, hear my oath ! I swear that never man born of woman has lain between my thighs save thou and this poor pilgrim that fell with me upon the river's bank. And I call on God to witness my oath and to prove my innocence by this red-hot iron ! "

The King replied : " It is enough. Bring hither the hot iron. May it please God to show thee innocent, according to the word of thy oath."

" Amen," said Iseult. And she boldly took the red-hot iron in her hand, and held it, showing neither fear nor pain. Thus it pleased God in His mercy to justify Iseult by the ordeal of fire.

And Iseult was reconciled to the king, who cast aside all his suspicion and was sorry that he had ever doubted Tristan. And all the riches of his kingdom seemed to Mark as nothing beside the love which he bare to Iseult.

CHAPTER ELEVEN

PETIT-CRÛ

NOW on the day of the ordeal by fire, Tristan left England, without waiting to hear the result, and took service with Duke Gilan of Wales.

And one day, when Tristan was sitting, sad and out of spirits, the Duke sent for his own favourite dog, to amuse and cheer him.

This dog was a magic dog; he came from the faery land of Avalon. He was so beautiful that no human tongue could describe him. On every side he gleamed with diverse hues. From before he appeared white, black and green; seen obliquely he was red like blood, as though his skin had been turned inside out; another way he seemed deep brown and at another angle pale rose-colour; but when he was looked at sideways it was impossible to tell his form and colour, for he seemed to have none. Never was there an animal so delicate, fine, clever, quick and obedient. His name was Petit-crû. And hung at his neck was a little golden bell which tinkled whenever he moved, with so sweet and magical a sound that it eased the heart of all earthly care. When Tristan heard it, he forgot his love, he forgot all his sorrow, he knew not where he was nor what he did ; he was filled with joy and content of mind at the melody of that wondrous bell.

Now Tristan felt that he would gladly lay down his life, if only he might send this dog to Iseult to ease her of her grief. But he knew that Gilan would never give up Petit-crû, and he could not think what to do.

It happened, however, that there was a certain giant called Urgan the Hairy, who lived beside the sea-shore and demanded every year a tithe of all the cattle and produce of the dukedom. So Tristan said to Duke Gilan :

" What will you give me, if I rid your land of the giant ? "

And Gilan promised to give him whatsoever he would.

Then Tristan took his horse and arms and went down to a bridge over the river. And there he met Urgan, who was just driving his stolen cattle home.

Tristan stood at the bridge-head and turned the cattle back. Then Urgan called out with a terrible voice :

" Who art thou, that hinderest my cattle from passing ? "

Then said he : " I am Tristan. I fear neither thee nor thy mighty club. Never again shalt thou take tribute from this country ! "

Then the giant rushed at Tristan, brandishing his huge and knotted club. Long and fierce was the fight, but at length Tristan overcame the giant and smote him so that he fled bellowing. But Tristan pursued him to his castle, and slew him; and so returned to Gilan bringing back the cattle and the hand of the giant in proof that he had killed him.

Then said Gilan : " Thou hast done well ; now claim thy recompense."

Tristan replied : " I pray thee, give me Petit-crû."

Gilan was surprised and said : " For thy brave deed I would gladly give thee half my dukedom, and my sister in marriage."

" Nay," said Tristan, " of all thy dukedom I want nothing but the one gift I have chosen.

> " For the sole sake of Petit-crû
> My hand the Hairy Urgan slew."

" If this be indeed thy choice," said the Duke, " I will give him to thee with pleasure."

Right glad was Tristan when he received Petit-crû. He called a courteous and trustworthy minstrel, and sent him to Tintagel to deliver Petit-crû to Iseult.

The queen received the gift with joy. She made a beautiful little kennel for Petit-crû and richly rewarded the minstrel. And wherever she went, whether riding or sleeping or sitting at meat, she had Petit-crû's kennel placed beside her, so that he might never be out of her sight.

But this was not for the comfort she drew from the magic bell, but for the love she bore to Tristan. When the sound of the sweet tinkling banished care from her heart, she thought only :

" Can I be carefree and content, while my love Tristan is full of sorrow ? Without me he lives wretchedly ; and shall I live happy when he is sad ? God forbid ! "

Then she tore the magic bell from Petit-crû's collar. And therewith the spell was broken and the bell lost all its virtue. Never again did its sound comfort men's hearts.

CHAPTER TWELVE

THE FOREST

MEANWHILE the minstrel had returned and told Tristan that Iseult and Mark were reconciled, and that all the king's suspicion against his nephew was turned to good-will. So Tristan returned with joy to Cornwall, and was received with kind welcome, and there he abode many days in joy and favour.

But how secretly and prudently soever the lovers bore themselves, the old suspicion began to raise its head again. The tongues of scandal-mongers, the cunning of spies, their own amorous glances betrayed them at every turn. Though Mark never surprised them together, yet he knew too well what to think. His brow grew dark with shame and grief; he could no longer abide it.

Therefore he called all the nobles of the court together and addressed his wife and nephew in their presence, saying that he could not suffer this scandal to go on. For compassion's sake, he would not put them to death; but he would banish them from his court and from his country to wander whithersoever they would.

Who now can tell the rapture of Tristan and
Iseult ? Hand in hand they departed, ravished
with bliss, and speechless.

They took twenty marks of gold from Iseult's
dower, and Tristan's harp and sword, his hunting-
horn and bow and his hound Hodain ; so they
left Tintagel and wandered away till they came
to a great, wild forest.

Nothing did they care what they should do for
food ; they trusted in God to provide. They
wanted nothing but what they had, since they had
one another. They found a deep cavern hewn
by giants aforetime in the living rock, and here
they made their dwelling. The entrance to the
cave was hidden, and approached only by a secret
way ; before it grew a great tree to shelter them
from the sun's heat in summer ; within, there was
a fair spring of clear water, and the whole floor of
the cavern was enamelled with gay and sweetly-
perfumed flowers. When it was bad weather, the
lovers took shelter in their cavern from the rain
and cold ; but when it was fair, they went forth
to take their pleasure beside the stream, or to hunt
for food in the forest round about. Tristan had
taught Hodain to hunt silently, without baying,
lest the sound betray them. And so they lived
together in utter happiness night and day, for they
had their desire.

But Mark, alone in his palace, grieved for the
loss of Iseult. And one day he went out hunting
as was his custom. And it happened that he and

a few of his huntsmen became separated from the main body, and followed two of the best hounds upon the track of a deer. The quarry fled through the forest till he came to the stream, and, plunging into the water, threw the hounds off the scent. The chief-huntsman made a cast to pick up the slot of the deer, and came upon a hidden path. He followed this to the cave and, looking in, saw Tristan and Iseult asleep, for the day was hot and they were weary. And it chanced, by God's will, that they were lying apart from one another, with Tristan's sword between them.

When the huntsman saw that, he trembled, and went and told the king. So Mark came to the cavern and saw them lying thus, and said :

"Surely I have been mistaken all this while. They are innocent, else would they not lie so, with the sword between them."

And as he looked upon Iseult, she seemed to him more fair than anything in the whole world. And a sunbeam pierced through an opening in the cave and fell on Iseult's cheek. Then Mark stepped softly to her and laid his glove upon her cheek, so gently that she did not wake. He departed, sadly and silently, and called his men together and rode away home without a word.

When Iseult woke, she found the glove upon her face, and recognised it for Mark's. Then they knew that Mark had found out their hiding-place.

But Mark summoned his court and told them

how he had found Tristan and Iseult sleeping innocently, and how he was convinced that all his former suspicions were untrue. And he sent to the forest and fetched Iseult home in peace and joy again.

But nothing could abate the power of the love-philtre or keep those lovers asunder. Again and again they met and gave rein to their desire. And one day, when they were together in the orchard, Tristan fell asleep. . . .

Here begins the Cambridge Fragment.

And in his arms Iseult the queen,
Full well they deemed themselves secure.
But hither by strange aventure,
Led by the dwarf, came Mark to watch
    them,
5   Expecting in their guilt to catch them.
But well for them, by God's pity
They found them sleeping harmlessly.
The king saw ; to the dwarf said he :
" Wait but a little here for me ;
10   Up to the palace I will go
To bring some barons here also,
How we have found them for to learn ;
When this is proven, they shall burn."

Now Tristan woke and saw the King ;
15   Yet gave no sign of anything,
Till to the palace Mark turned back.

Then Tristan rose and spake : " Alack,
Sweet love Iseult, wake up anon,
We have been trapped and spied upon !
20 The king knows all that we have wrought,
Goes now to fetch his lords from court ;
In company he will us take
To judge and burn us at the stake.
Sweet heart, I must depart from thee ;
25 Thy life is in no jeopardy,
Since proof of this they will have none
[If they shall find thee here alone.
To far-off lands, in bitter woe,
For thy love's sake I fain must go,]*
Leave all my joy, become a stranger,
Renounce delight and follow danger.
Such grief it is from thee to sever
30 I shall no more feel joy for ever.
My most sweet lady, this I pray :
Never forget me any day ;
Far off from thee, yet hold me dear
As e'er thou didst when I was near.
35 Lady, I dare no longer stay ;
Kiss me before I go away."

Iseult to kiss him yet withheld,
She heard his speech, his tears beheld,
Wept from her eyes, from heart she
    sighed ;

---

* These three lines, missing from the MS., have been conjecturally restored by M. Bédier, from the parallel passage
in the *Saga*.

40   " Fair sir and friend," she softly cried,
      " Remember well this bitter morrow
      That severed us with so much sorrow.
      This parting grieveth me so sore
      I ne'er knew what grief was before ;
45   Now no more joy for me is left,
      Since of thy comfort I'm bereft,
      Pity nor tenderness of heart
      If from thy love I have to part.
      Needs must our bodies sunder thus,
50   But none can part the love of us.
      Nevertheless, my lover, take
      This ring, and keep it for my sake. . .

The End of the Cambridge Fragment.

. . . and let it be a token of love between thee and me forever."

So in great sorrow they parted, tenderly weeping and embracing one another. And when the king returned with his barons, they found the queen alone. Nor would the barons believe the king's story, but persuaded him to take her back.

CHAPTER THIRTEEN

THE MARRIAGE OF TRISTAN

NOW Tristan went away sorrowful to his lodging and called his attendants together. They took ship and fled the kingdom. Through many lands did Tristan wander, seeking adventure. He stayed a little while in Normandy; he served a long time under the Emperor of Rome; then he visited Spain; and afterwards returned to Armenye and was received with great joy by Roald le Foytenant.

Now at that time there was an aged duke ruling in Brittany, whose land was harried by many enemies. He had a son named Kaherdin, a brave and courteous knight, who became great friends with Tristan. Tristan was invited to Brittany, and given a fair castle for his own; and he helped the duke in his wars, vanquishing all his enemies and freeing the country from raids and invasions.

Now Kaherdin had a sister, fair, courteous and well-advised beyond any maiden of the land. And she was called Iseult of the White Hands.

Whenever Tristan heard her name, he thought upon that other Iseult, Iseult of Ireland; and

because of the name Iseult, his heart was troubled
and his eyes grew tender when he looked upon her.

And he composed many lays of love, with words
cunningly linked, whereof the refrain ran ever :

> Iseult my love, Iseult my wife,
> In thee my death, in thee my life!

Now when Tristan sang these lays before Iseult
of the White Hands and her parents, all who
listened thought that he was singing them to her
and that he had no other Iseult in mind. They
were all overjoyed, especially Kaherdin, who did
all he could to bring about a marriage between his
sister and his friend Tristan. And as Tristan
was often in the maiden's company, she grew to
love him with all her virgin heart. In Tristan too,
there grew up a kind of longing and restless ache
of love. Whenever he thought of Iseult of
Ireland, he was filled with remorse ; yet, when he
saw the beauty and gentle manners of Iseult of
Brittany, he yearned after her. The desire of his
soul was for Iseult of Ireland ; but the will of his
body was strong within him and gave him no peace.

Here begins the first Sneyd Fragment.

> This way and that he turns his mind
> Still striving some new shift to find,
> 55 Whereby he now may change his will
> Since his desire he can't fulfil.
> And so he says, " Iseult, fair friend,
> How diversely our lives we spend !

So fades thy love away and leaves me,
60 It turns to nothing and deceives me.
For thee I put away delight,
Which thou hast both by day and night ;
In bitter grief my life doth move,
And thine in the delights of love.
65 Nought can I do but long for thee,
But thou canst fail not verily
To dwell in great delight and pleasure,
And do thy will in fullest measure.
While for thy flesh my body aches
70 The king with thee his pleasure takes :
Therein he findeth joy and bliss,
That which was mine, to-day is his.
I'll claim not what may not be had,
For well I know that she is glad ;
75 She has forgot me in her mirth.
While I all other maids on earth
Despise for her, Iseult, alone.
And comfort she will give me none,
Though well she knows the bitter ache
80 Of love I suffer for her sake.
Another maid desires me sore,
Whereby my anguish is the more ;
Were I of love importuned less
I better might endure love's stress.
85 Yet by this chase, save she give heed,
I may perchance of love be freed.
Since of desire I am bereft
I can but turn to what is left ;
I must, methinks—for every man

90   May only grasp what things he can.
        What boots to make this long delay,
        All joy forswearing day by day,
        Still cherishing a love which could
        At no time come to any good ?
95   Yea, for her love I did sustain
        So much of grief, so much of pain,
        May I not now be done with it ?
        To cherish it avails no whit,
        Since she has clean forgotten me,
100   And changed her whole heart utterly.
        O God in Heaven, Father fair,
        How might this change be wrought in her ?
        How could she change, when on my side
        Love doth unchangeably abide ?
105   How could she set aside her love ?
        For I can get no peace thereof.
        Yea, if her heart from me should turn,
        Surely, by hers my own would learn ;
        She could do nothing, well or ill,
110   Without my heart should know it still.
        My heart to me most surely saith
        That hers hath kept me utter faith,
        And, as it might, has succoured me.
        Though my desire I may not see,
115   I ought not therefore to turn ranger
        Nor thus desert her for a stranger.
        For we have borne too much for love,
        Too long in love our bodies strove,
        That I, being let in my desire,
120   Should any other maid require.

Whereas, for all Iseult might do,
Will hath she, but no power, thereto ;
Nor must I cherish evil mood
Against her, while her will is good,
125   Though of my will she make me lack ;
I know not what doth hold her back.
Iseult, whate'er thy power may be,
A right good will thou hast to me.
For how then could she e'er remove ?
130   I cannot cheat her of my love ;
Should there be change upon her part
I know, I'd learn it by my heart,
Treason or none, I cannot tell,
That there's a breach, I know too well ;
135   Deep in my heart abides this thought
Her love for me is small or nought.
If in her heart her love did live
Some little comfort she would give.
—Comfort, whereof ?—Of this my pain.
140   —Finding me where ?—Where I remain.
—She knows not where, in what country.
—Eh ! let her seek the world for me !
—Wherefore ?—To comfort my despair.
—For her lord's sake she would not dare,
145   Though she willed well toward me still.
Nay, without power, what boots goodwill ?
Let her love Mark and to him cling,
I crave not her remembering ;
I blame her not if she forget me,
150   She ought not pining to regret me ;
With her great beauty 'tis not fit,

Nor doth her nature order it,
That she, while Mark her love can sate,
Should languish for another mate,
155 She in the king should take delight
So great, as to forget me quite,
And in her lord such pleasure find
As drives her lover from her mind.
What can my love to her afford,
160 Weighed 'gainst her pleasure in her lord?
Yea, she must bow to nature's hest,
Since of her will she's dispossessed.
Let her hold fast to what she may
Since she her love must put away;
165 What she may have, let her hold fast,
Till it become her will at last.
By loving play, by many a kiss
One may be reconciled to this.
Soon he will cause her such good glee
170 She will remember nought of me.
Let her forget! What should I rue?
I care not if well or ill she do.
She may have pleasure and delight
Surely, methinks, in love's despite.
175 In love's despite—Nay! how could she
E'er with her lord taste love or glee?
How could she evermore forget
A thing so deep in memory set?
How can man's will be ever moved
180 To have in hate what he has loved,
Or ever carry hate and ire
Thither, where he hath set desire?

What he hath loved he cannot hate.
Natheless, he may withdraw him straight,
185 And turn away, and far remove,
When he sees no good cause to love.
Both hate and love he ought to shun
If he should find good cause for none.
He that doth deeds of good report
190 Mingled with deeds of baser sort,
His nobler acts we ought to weigh
And never ill for ill repay.
The one the other so alloys,
The two things hang in counterpoise ;
195 Not too much love, because of ill,
Nor, for good's sake, too much ill-will,
Since love is due to what is good,
But evil ought to be withstood.
For the good's sake I will not hate,
200 Nor, for the evil, on her wait.
Because Iseult once loved me so,
And semblance of such joy did show,
I must not hate her now at all,
For anything that may befall.
205 But since she casts her love behind
I ought to put her from my mind,
Must neither love her any more,
Nor bear her any hate therefore ;
But I will draw my heart away,
210 As she has done, if so I may,
And work and deed I will employ
To see if I can win me joy,
By that same deed in love's despite

Wherein with Mark she finds delight.
215 How can the thing be better tried
Than taking to myself a bride?
Sure, for this bridal were no need
Were she not wife to him indeed,
But she to him is truly wed
220 By whom our love was severèd.
From him she cannot draw away,
Whate'er her will, she must obey,
No such compulsion suffer I,
Yet how she lives I fain would try.
225 And I will take the maid to wife,
And taste a little Iseult's life,
If marriage, and if amorous play
Will put her from my heart away,
Even as she her joy doth take
230 With Mark, and all our love forsake.
It is not hate that urgeth me;
Simply I would of her be free,
Repay the love the maid doth bring,
To see how Iseult loves the king."

235 Tristan in anguish seeks to see
What end of this new love may be,
In torment great and strife of mind,
No other reason can he find
But that this trial he doth require:
240 If he may glad him 'gainst desire,
And in this joy on which he's set
The other Iseult may forget,
Thinking that she forgets him quite

For her lord's sake and for delight.
245 A lawful wife he'll take ; that so
Iseult no blame on him may throw
For seeking pleasure lawlessly
Or shaming his nobility :
He seeks Iseult of White-hand fame
250 For her fair face and Iseult's name.
Ne'er for the beauty found in her
Save she the name Iseult did bear,
Nor for the name without the face,
Had he desired to do her grace.
255 But for these two things in her found
Is he upon this emprise bound,
That he the gentle maid will wed
To set himself in the queen's stead,
To see how he may pleasure take
260 In love toward a wedded make.
He seeks himself to try the thing
That Iseult worketh with the king,
Therefore to try he is full fain
What joy he may with Iseult gain.
265 Thus for his dole, thus for his grief,
Tristan in vengeance seeks relief ;
He seeks such vengeance for his trouble
As will but make his torment double ;
He of his torment will be quit
270 And only heaps up more of it.
He thinks to have delight herein,
Since to his will he may not win.
The queen's own name and goodlihead
Tristan hath noted in the maid ;

275   He would not wed for that sole name,
Nor for the face without that same;
Were she not Iseult called, then ne'er
Had Tristan looked with love on her;
Had not she had Iseult's fair face,
280   Tristan had never shown her grace.
For the name's sake and lovely mien
That Tristan in the maid hath seen,
He comes the maiden to require
Both in his will and his desire.

285   Hark to a strange adventure then!
Marvellous are the hearts of men,
In every place unfixed of will,
They are by nature mutable;
They will not leave their evil mood,
290   Yet easily they change the good.
Such habit of ill-deeds they make
That ill for good they oft mistake;
They are so used to all that's base
They know not what is nobleness,
295   They are so set on villainy,
They clean forget their courtesy;
They take such pains to compass wrong,
They dwell therein their whole life long,
Of ill they cannot get them quit,
300   So throughly are they steeped in it.
With some, ill-deeds their custom be;
Others seek virtue waveringly.
And all their life their hankering
Is only after some new thing,

305　They weary of their powers for good
　　And truckle to their baser mood.
　　Their wandering fancy quickly tires
　　And quits good powers for lewd desires ;
　　They leave the good they might have had
310　To find delight in what is bad.
　　A man will let his own goods go
　　To snatch his neighbour's, good or no,
　　His own possessions he despises,
　　While other's envied wealth he prizes.
315　If what he has were not his own
　　He'd keep it fain, and make no moan,
　　But what falls rightly to his part
　　He cannot value in his heart.
　　Were he deprived of what he's got,
320　His chase thereafter would be hot,
　　But better things he thinks to find,
　　And therefore hates it in his mind.
　　For fickleness is but a cheat,
　　Which makes him thus despise what's
　　　　meet,
325　The thing he hath not, coveting,
　　And leave his own for a worse thing.
　　Let him eschew ill-deeds who may,
　　Put, for good's sake, the worse away,
　　Seek wisdom and leave foolishness,
330　For it is never fickleness
　　To change in order to amend,
　　Or flee from uses that offend.
　　But many a man runs after change,
　　And thinks to find in what is strange

335   That which he cannot find at home ;
      And all this sets his thoughts to roam.
      What they have not, they long to try,
      Only to weary by and by.
      And on such wise do women use,
340   Leave what they have for what they choose,
      And seek how they may come until
      Their own desire and their own will.
      Certes, I speak I know not what,
      But men and women both have got
345   Too great an itch for novelty,
      And change their mind too easily,
      And change desire, and change their will
      Clean against reason and their skill.
      This man by loving seeks to gain,
350   And nothing gets of it but pain ;
      And *that* seeks to be rid of love,
      And gets but double grief thereof ;
      Another loud for vengeance calls,
      And soon to sad repentance falls ;
355   Another thinks to win relief,
      And doth but pile up grief on grief.

      Tristan from Iseult thought to part,
      And tear the love out from his heart ;
      He takes the one Iseult to wife
360   To thrust that other from his life.
      Had that first Iseult never been
      He'd not love this Iseult, I ween ;
      But for that first love Iseult's sake
      A new Iseult he longs to take ;

365 Since that Iseult may not be his,
He sets his will on having this ;
If he Queen Iseult might have wed
He had not loved Iseult the maid.
Therefore, methinks I well can prove
370 This was not wrath, and yet not love.
Had it been love, the fine, the pure,
Surely he never could endure,
Loving the maid, his love to slight.
But yet, pure hate it was not quite,
375 Since, urged by the queen's love alone,
He took the maiden for his own.
Since for her love he took this mate
Surely for her he felt no hate.
Hating Iseult, he could not take
380 Iseult to wife for Iseult's sake.
Yet, had his love been utter-fine,
To wed Iseult he'd not incline.
But on this wise his fortune wrought,
That he by love was so distraught
385 That he must strive, in love's despite,
To be of love delivered quite ;
Seeking to be of sorrow quit
He plunged him deeper into it.
With many men it falleth so,
390 When love hath brought them grievous
        woe,
Pain, anguish, contrariety,
They, striving but to set them free,
To venge them and deliver them,
To heavier loads themselves condemn,

395   And often with their wits devise
       Schemes that increase their miseries.
       I've seen it hap to many a one,
       When of his will he is undone,
       And cannot have the thing he would,
400   Then he has taken what he could;
       To such a deed distress doth urge him,
       Whereby his grief the more doth scourge him,
       And when to rid him he is fain
       He never can get free again.

405   In vengeance wrought on such a wise
       Both love and wrath I recognise;
       Nor love nor hatred here is single;
       Both wrath with love doth intermingle,
       And love with wrath is mingled too.
410   Who doth the thing he would not do,
       Because his wish he mayn't acquire,
       He works his will against desire;
       And Tristan does on this wise still:
       Against desire he works his will;
415   For where Iseult hath caused him pain
       He would by Iseult solace gain.
       He gives caresses, kisses such,
       And with her parents speaks so much,
       That to this marriage all agree,
420   They to bestow, to take her, he.

       They fix the time, the day they name.
       By friends attended, Tristan came;
       There is the duke with his meinie;
       All preparations ready be;

425 And thus White-hand Iseult he wed.
The chaplain all the Bride-mass said,
And what to service appertains,
As rite of Holy Church ordains.
Then did they revel at the feast,
430 And next made merry as they pleased
At the quintain and the mellay,
With javelins and darts they play,
At wrestling and at fence they vie
In various games of rivalry,
435 As in such feasts is right and fit
And the world's fashion orders it.

The day speeds past with its delight ;
The beds are ready made for night.
There to her bed they bring the maid,
440 And Tristan gets him disarrayed
The meanwhile, of his wedding-vest ;
Close-fitting 'twas, and tight at wrist.
And pulling, as the sleeve doth cling,
Forth of his hand they pull the ring
445 Iseult gave in the garden there
The last day that he spake with her.
Tristan looks down ; sees the ring plain,
And all his mind is changed again ;
A mighty grief on him doth fall,
450 He knows not what to do at all,
For clean beyond his power it is
To carry through his will in this,
And strictly now he broods thereon
Till he repents the deed he's done.

455   His deed is treason to his heart
And in his soul he shrinks apart;
The ring that on his finger sits
Makes him distracted in his wits.
Then he recalls the oath he sware
460   In that day when he went from her
And in the garden took his leave;
From deepest heart a sigh doth heave.
" How can I do it ? " then saith he,
" 'Tis clean against the heart of me;
465   Yet it behoves me share the bed
With her, as with my wife well-wed;
And with her I am bound to lie,
And not desert, nor pass her by;
My foolish heart of all is cause,
470   That still so light and fickle was,
When I to win the maiden's hand
Of friends and parents made demand.
Little of Love Iseult I thought
When I this foolish fancy caught
475   To cheat my love, my faith forswear.
Yet must I lie with her, howe'er
It irk me, for I wed her truly
In all men's eyes, by Church-rite duly:
I cannot set her now aside,
480   And by my folly must abide,
Since without much ill-deed and sin
I cannot well draw back herein,
Nor join myself in love with her
Unless by turning perjurer.
485   So far to that Iseult I gave me,

That 'tis unreason this should have me.
So much to this Iseult I owe
I must to that my faith forego.
My faith I ought not to betray,
490 Nor yet this Iseult put away.
Iseult my lady I despite
If e'er in this I take delight,
And yet, if I from this refrain,
I do foul wrong and sin and bane ;
495 To leave her now is nowise right,
Nor yet to take with her delight
By lying with her in her bed
For my own mirth and joyous stead.
So far with Queen Iseult went I
500 That with the maid I must not lie,
Yet with the maid so far have gone
As now I can't go back upon.
Queen Iseult I must not deceive ;
Nor yet my wife I must not leave,
505 To part from her were no way meet ;
Nor to lie with her 'neath the sheet.
If to my wife I keep my oath
I to Iseult have broken troth,
And if to Iseult I am loyal
510 Faith to my wife I quite despoil.
My faith I would not set at nought,
Nor yet against Iseult do aught.
Which shall I injure of the two ?
Treason to one I needs must do,
515 And fraud, and treachery and pain,
Or else I must betray the twain.

So close to me I've brought the maid,
Iseult already I've betrayed;
And, for I loved the queen so long,
520   Already done the maiden wrong.
And more than all am I tricked too!
In an ill hour both these I knew;
Both these for me are grievèd deep,
I for a double Iseult weep;
525   Yea, both by me have been undone,
And needs must I be false to one.
Faith to Queen Iseult kept I not,
Nor can I keep it now, I wot,
To her for whom I brake my vow.
530   To *one* I yet may keep it now!
Though to the queen I've been untrue
Faith to the maid at least is due,
For certainly I cannot leave her—
Nor to the other be deceiver.
535   Surely I know not how to act,
In every way I am distract:
To keep my faith is bitter strife,
Yet worse 'tis to desert my wife.
Let joy, let grief thereof betide
540   I must go lay me at her side.
I'm so revenged on Iseult's sin
I first am taken in the gin;
My vengeance is so well rehearsed
I in the trap am taken first.
545   My spite has pulled on my own head
Such woes as leave me hard bested.
If I should lie with this my spouse

'Twill Iseult's bitter wrath arouse,
Yet if from her I lie aloof
550   It shall be turned to my reproof,
And all *her* wrath will fall on me ;
Of all her friends and family
I should but win the hate and scorn,
And before God I were forsworn.
555   Both shame and sin alike I dread ;
Therefore, when I am come to bed,
Save I do that I most abhor,
Which doth my conscience grieve full sore
And goes against my heart outright,
560   I'll of my bed have no delight,
She'll know by what I leave undone
I more desire another one,
Simple is she if she guess not
Another my best love has got,
565   And that to lie I were full fain
Where greater joys I might obtain.
Save she shall have her joy of me,
Little, methinks, her love will be ;
She would have reason good for hating
570   Did I withhold that natural mating
Which ought in love to make us one ;
For love disprized breeds hate anon.
For as love comes from mating, so
From abstinence must hatred grow ;
575   And thus love springs from love's delight,
But hatred out of love's despite.
If I withhold myself from her
My grief shall be the heavier,

And all my prowess and my fame
580   Turn but to cowardice and shame.
What I have won by my renown
Now by this love will be cast down,
And all the love she had for me
By my refusal lost will be ;
585   My service, and my valour's boast,
By cowardice shall all be lost.
She loved me when she had me not,
And longed for me in heart, I wot ;
She'll hate me now if I refrain
590   And make that sweet desiring vain,
Which still the strongest bond doth prove
Lover and loved to knit in love.
Therefore I will not do this deed,
Rather of love I'd have her freed ;
595   Better that she should hate me sore,
Hate, and not love, I covet more,
And now indeed it falls on me.
I to my love did treachery,
Who loved me more than any man.
600   Therefore this will in me began,
Yea, and this longing, this requiring,
And this fierce stress, and this desiring
I had, to know the maiden here ;
So that at last I wedded her,
605   Against my love, against my troth
Due unto Iseult by my oath.
I shall be found more faithless yet
The closer to my wife I get.
Though by my speech I seek excuse

610 By sleight of tongue, and shift, and ruse,
    For faith to Iseult perjurèd,
    I do but seek this woman's bed.
    I seek excuse in love's despite
    In this new mate to take delight.
615 While Iseult lives, I must not break
    Faith to my love for my lust's sake ;
    I play the part of treachour base
    To chase for love to her disgrace ;
    So far already I have run
620 That woe is me till life is done.
    So, as I've wronged my love, I vow
    She shall have justice from me now,
    And penance will I undergo
    Because I have deservèd so.
625 So in this bed I will me lay,
    But will abstain from all love's play ;
    No torment, sure, could I devise
    To give more constant miseries,
    Or greater pain to me supply,
630 Let love, let hate betwixt us lie.
    For if it yearn me to enjoy her
    'Twill grieve me sore not to employ her ;
    And if I not desire this glee,
    Bitter will be her bed to me.
635 Therefore, I think, come love, come hate,
    I must endure a torment great ;
    Since I to Iseult troth did break
    This penance on myself I take,
    And when she knows what straits I'm in
640 I shall have pardon for my sin."

Tristan lies in Iseult's embrace,
She kisses both his mouth and face,
And draws him close, deep sighs doth heave,
Longing for that he will not give ;
645   Contrary to his will it is
To seek, or to renounce, his bliss,
Since nature fain would have her way,
But Iseult doth his reason sway.
Him his desire towards the queen
650   From will toward the maid doth wean,
Desire so holdeth will in thrall
That nature has no power at all ;
Reason and love constrain him so
His body's will they quite o'erthrow.
655   Yea, for Iseult his mighty love
His natural will doth clean remove,
And slays that will and craving thought
Which 'gainst desire upon him wrought.
He had good will his joy to gain,
660   But love doth greatly him restrain.
He knows her fair, he feels her kind,
Loves joy and hates love in his mind,
For if desire were any less,
Then he might yield to his will's stress,
665   But now he yields him to desire.
He is in torment and on fire,
And in great grief and in great pain,
He knows not how he shall refrain,
Nor what words to his wife shall use,
670   Nor by what sleight himself excuse.
Natheless some shame upon him wrought,

He flees the thing that once he sought,
His pleasures doth avoid and flee,
And of her body gets no glee.
675 Then : " Fairest love," did Tristan say,
" Think not the worse of me I pray
If now a secret I reveal
And beg you straitly to conceal,
That none may know it save we two,
680 'Twas ne'er to any told but you.
Know that upon my right-hand side
My body doth a sickness hide
That now long time hath holden me ;
To-night it pains me grievously.
685 All the great toils that I have done
Makes it throughout my body run.
It keepeth me in such sore pain,
And so my vital parts doth gain
I dare not love's delight to take,
690 Nor yet exert me, for its sake ;
For never did I so before
But that I fainted three times o'er,
And after, long lay sick, I wot.
If I refrain now, blame me not.
695 We shall have times for pleasure still
When thou and I alike shall will."
" Thy pain," said Iseult, " grieves me more
Than any grief the wide world o'er ;
As for the rest whereof you tell,
700 Without it I can do full well."

Within her room Iseult doth sigh,

Desiring Tristan wearily;
No other way her thought can turn
But still on Tristan's love to yearn,
705 No other will her mind can move,
No other hope, no other love;
On him her whole desire is set.
Yet she of him no news can get,
Where he may be, or far or near,
710 Living or dead, she cannot hear.
Therefore she dwells in deeper sorrow
To get no word for many a morrow.
She knows not he is in Bretayn,
Rather believes him still in Spain,
715 The land where he the giant slew
Was nephew to great Orgoilleu,
That rode to seek, from Afric's strand,
Princes and kings in many a land.
Orgoilleu was a hardy wight,
720 With each and all of them did fight,
Many a one did mate and slay,
Shore from their chins the beard away,
Wove of the beards a mantle wide,
Trailing, and huge from side to side.
725 Then he heard tell of Arthur's name
That in all lands had so much fame,
Such hardihood, such valiantness,
He never was o'erthrown in press,
But still with many a foe had fought
730 And all to utter downfall brought.
Now when the giant heard of it,
As to a friend he lets him wit

That he had made a mantle new,
(But lacking cord and fringe thereto),
735 Of beards of kings and barons high
And lords of many a country nigh,
Whom he in war had made to yield
Or slain upon the battle-field,
Weaving thereof a weed as rare
740 As might be wrought of royal hair ;
Natheless, the fringe was lacking yet.
So, seeing Arthur highest set,
Above all kings in worth and land,
He for his love's sake made demand
745 That Arthur now his beard should trim
And, for his honour, send to him ;
For he would do him this great grace,
High o'er the rest his beard to place.
As Arthur ruled the world's domain,
750 Above all kings lord suzerain,
So Arthur's beard he would uplift,
(If he would shear it as a gift),
Set it in highest place above
And make the cord and fringe thereof.
755 But if to send he should refuse
He'd do with him as he did use,
Cloak against beard would set at stake
And deadly war on Arthur make,
So let him take that should prevail
760 Both beard and mantle without fail.

When all this tale King Arthur heard
Both grief and rage within him stirred ;

He to the giant answer sent :
That war were rather his intent
765 Than that his beard he should off-shear
To send him, out of coward fear.
Whereat the giant, when he learned
The answer that the king returned,
Invaded straight, to seek him out,
770 His country's marches round about,
Battle against him for to wage.
They met together to engage,
Bringing both cloak and beard for prize,
And fought in fierce and wrathful wise.
775 Encounter hard and deadly fray
They held together all one day.
Next morn King Arthur conquerèd,
Took both the giant's cloak and head,
By prowess and by hardihood
780 Vanquished him thus in manner good.

This to the tale importeth not,—
Yet I must let you know, God wot,
Our giant nephew was to him
Who used those kingly beards to trim.
785 Now from the king and emperor
For whom Sir Tristan armour bore,
Then whenas he was yet in Spain
Before he journeyed to Bretayn,
He did demand the beard likewise.
790 To give it up the king denies ;
Yet in his land from end to end
Finds not a kinsman nor a friend

His beard's defence to take in hand
And with the giant in combat stand.
795 Much was the king cast down in soul,
Before his court he made his dole ;
Tristan the deed did undertake,
Fierce war on his behalf did make
And battle bitter to abide.
800 Great were the hurts on either side.
Tristan was wounded grievously,
Sore wounds into his side had he,
His friends were set in grievous pain ;
The giant, ne'ertheless, was slain.
805 Since this hard hap, Iseult had heard
Of Tristan not one single word.
Such wont has envy ever had :
To say of good, nought, much of bad ;
For envy doth good deeds conceal,
810 But evil deeds will still reveal.
Therefore the Sage in antique writ
Counsels his son because of it :
" 'Tis better to be comradeless
Than envious comrade to possess,
815 Better no comrade, night or day,
Than one that loves you not, I say.
He'll hide the good thing that he knows,
And out of hate the ill disclose ;
If one do well, he'll ne'er reveal it.
820 If ill, he will from none conceal it.
Far better then no friend at all
Than one whence nought but ill doth fall."
Tristan hath comrades many enough

That bear him hate and little love ;
825 About King Mark stands many a one
That bears him faith and friendship none.
These tell Iseult no good report,
But spread ill-tidings through the court ;
They are full loth the good to know
830 Because the queen desires it so,
And, for their envy is so great,
Loudly they speak what she doth hate.

She in her chamber sat one day
Making of love a piteous lay.
835 How Guiron was surprised and ta'en,
And for his lady's love was slain,
Whom he more loved than all alive.
And how the count did after give
Sir Guiron's heart, by wicked cheat,
840 Unto his wife one day to eat,
And of the lady's dolorous cry
At learning how her love did die.

Sweetly and well the lady sings,
The voice accordeth with the strings,
845 Fair are the hands, the lay also,
Sweet is the voice, the singing low,
When Cariado thither went,
A noble count, and rich in rent,
With castles fair and wide estate.
850 He to the court had come to wait
Upon the queen, her love to get ;
Iseult made but a mock of it,
Yet many a time he'd made demand

Since that that other left the land.
855 Thither he came his court to pay,
But still could bear no gain away,
Nor win so much of Iseult's love
As 'twere the value of a glove;
Whether in promise or in fee
860 No jot nor tittle e'er gat he.
Long time was he by love detained,
And many days in court remained.
A right fair knight he was, I ween,
Courteous and proud and well-beseen,
865 But yet deserved a lesser meed
Of praise, for arms and knightly deed.
He of fair speech was well possessed,
Gallant in love and quick in jest,
He found Iseult that sang her lay
870 And laughing, thus began to say:
"Well know I, dame, the owl's heard singing
When news of death is in the bringing,
Death of her song the burden is.
This song of yours, as well I wis,
875 The owl's own death doth signify,
For one there is that's doomed to die."
"Well hast thou said," Iseult replied,
"I grant the owl's death signified;
Well may that man be called an owl
880 Who frightens all men by his howl;
Your death it is you ought to fear
When death in this my song you hear,
For you indeed the owl may be
For all the news you bring to me.

885 Never have you told tidings here
Whereof I might have any cheer,
Nor ever yet my presence sought
But you some evil tale have brought.
And it is with you even so
890 As with the sluggard long ago,
Who'd never stir from his hearth-stone
Save to annoy or vex someone.
So you your lodging will not leave
Save you learn something that may grieve,
895 That you may blab it all about.
You will not stir to go far out
For any cause a man may name ;
Never of you went any fame,
To honour you in your friends' eyes
900 Nor to distress your enemies.
You prate of deeds that others do,
None will be chronicled of you ! "

Thus Cariado made reply :
" Now are you wroth, I know not why.
905 Who's scared at you, the more fool he !
Am I the he-owl ?   You're the she !
Howe'er *my* death may be decreed,
For *you* I have ill-news indeed
About Tristan, your lover true :
910 Dame Iseult, he is lost to you,
He's wed a wife in foreign place.
Henceforth you may for love go chase,
For he your love doth clean disdain,
And in great pomp a wife has ta'en,

915 Heir to the Duke of Brittany."
 Iseult makes answer angrily :
 " You've been an owlet every day
 Ill of Sir Tristan still to say !
 God do to me, and worse things too,
920 If I be not an owl for you !
 You have now brought me evil news ;
 All good to you I here refuse :
 I tell you sooth, your love is vain,
 Ne'er shall you get my grace again ;
925 You and your wooing I'll despise
 While light of life is in mine eyes.
 Ill had I chased, in very truth
 If I had ta'en your love, forsooth !
 To lose his love doth honour me
930 Far more than to accept from thee.
 Yea, hast thou brought an evil tale ?
 It shall full little thee avail ! "

 Great anger in Iseult doth swell
 As Cariado hears full well ;
935 He seeks no further speech to sting,
 Nor jests for her worse angering,
 But from the chamber swift doth go.
 Then is Iseult in utter woe,
 And at the news feels deadly smart
940 And bitter anger in her heart.
  The End of the Sneyd Fragment.

And Iseult wept, saying : "Never let any
woman trust a man more. Even Tristan is forsworn, and has taken a strange woman to wife."

Now Tristan and his friend Kaherdin won great honour and renown in the dukedom of Brittany, waging war and conquering towns and castles. Yet all this while, Tristan suffered sorrow and pain for Queen Iseult's sake.

On the marches of Brittany there was a great forest, which belonged to a giant named Moldagog. One day, when Tristan was out hunting, he separated himself from his companions and went in search of the giant. After fording a deep and perilous river, he came to the forest, and there he sounded his horn. Moldagog came rushing out with his club, crying in a rage :

"Who art thou ? And what dost thou in my forest ? "

Tristan replied :

"I am Tristan, son-in-law to the Duke of Brittany. I see that thou hast here a fine forest, secret and remote, fit for a purpose I have in mind. I wish to build a house here. Give me therefore forty-eight of the tallest and fairest trees wherewith to build it."

Then said Moldagog : "Fellow, over-boldness hath made thee mad ! Get thee hence, and be thankful that I let thee escape with thy life ! "

"Never ! " said Tristan. "I will fight with thee, and then I will take what trees I like."

So they fought ; and by a mighty blow Tristan cut off the giant's leg. At this, Moldagog threw away his club and begged for mercy, promising to serve Tristan and give him all his treasures.

Then Tristan made a wooden leg for Moldagog ; and he left him his castle and all his treasure, requiring only that the giant should furnish him with the house he wanted and say nought thereof to any man. So Tristan returned home, but spoke no word of his adventure.

Now in the midst of the forest there was a wondrous cave, hollowed in the living rock, and adorned with marvellous sculptures of beasts and birds and foliage. It had been made by a certain giant, that had aforetime been slain by King Arthur, at the time of his wars against the Emperor Lucius of Rome, but this story belongs not to our tale. Moldagog had this cave set in order, and sent for cunning workmen to carry out Tristan's wishes.

So Tristan came every day in secret to the cave, and let make a wondrous vault, coloured and painted with beautiful designs, and studded with precious stones, which were supplied by Moldagog. All the work was done by the workmen in secret, and carried in and set in place by Tristan and Moldagog. In the centre of the vault was set an image, so marvellously wrought in every limb, that it seemed to breathe with life, and so beauteous that there was nothing in the world to compare with it. In the breast of the image, Tristan set a hidden casket filled with spices and aromatic herbs, which exhaled exquisite odours through golden pipes, leading to the mouth and the nape of the image. And this image was in beauty and stature and shape the living portrait of Queen

Iseult. It was robed in a gown of queenly magnificence; on its head was a crown of gold and in its hand a sceptre, with a jewelled bird upon the tip, which fluttered its wings as though it were alive. The robe was of purple, to signify mourning, because of the sorrow Iseult suffered for Tristan's love. On the left hand was a ring, on which were written the words that Iseult had spoken to Tristan when they parted in the orchard : " Love Tristan, take this ring and wear it for my sake." Under the feet of the image was the figure of the wicked dwarf, and close beside was Petit-crû, who seemed to shake his head and sound his magic bell. And on the other side was a little image of Brangwain, dressed in a fair robe. In her hand she held a covered flask, and round about the lip were written these words : " Queen Iseult, drink this potion "; and this was the love-philtre which had been brewed in Ireland for King Mark.

On one side of the entrance to the cave, Tristan placed the image of a terrible giant, clothed in skins, and brandishing a mighty club, as though to slay all comers. On the other side was a great lion, cunningly wrought in copper so that he seemed alive. He stood upright on his feet, lashing his tail, over an image made in the likeness of the evil seneschal Mariadoc, who had betrayed Tristan to King Mark. And when Tristan had finished all these images, he locked the door of the vault and kept the keys, and commanded Moldagog to guard the cave so that none might enter.

So Tristan returned to the castle, and ate and drank and slept by the side of Iseult his wife, and behaved as usual with his companions, so that no one suspected anything. Iseult of the White Hands wondered greatly where he had been and what he had been doing, and why he would not have intercourse with her as a husband should, but she was so prudent and well-taught that she said nothing of all this to her kinsfolk and friends. And from time to time, Tristan went by secret ways to the cave. And when he beheld the image of Queen Iseult, he kissed and embraced it, as though it were his living love indeed. . . .

Here begins the First Turin Fragment.

And all their mighty love's delight,
Their travail and their dolorous plight,
Their grieving and their plaint as well
Doth Tristan to the image tell ;
945 Kisses it oft when he is glad,
Is wroth with it when he's so mad
To trust in brooding and in dream
Or in the lying heart of him,
And think she hath her love forsaken,
950 Or hath some other lover taken ;
That she her will cannot restrain
But of some other love is fain
That readier lies to hand for her.
This thought now causeth him to err,
955 Error doth hunt away his heart,
His doubts to Cariado start,

Lest unto him her love should stray ;
He is about her night and day,
He sings her praise, he serves her whim
960 And blameth her concerning him.
He fears lest, losing what she would,
She may have seized whate'er she could,
And, since she may not have Tristan,
Taken for love some other man.
965 When thus his wrath within him glows
He to the image hatred shows,
He will not then so much as view it,
Nor look at it, nor speak unto it,
Rather addresses thus Brangwain :
970 " To you, fair maiden, I complain
Of this foul change and treachery
Iseult my love hath put on me ! "
He to the image speaketh out
His thoughts ; then turns himself about
975 Till Iseult's hand he doth behold
Tendering him the ring of gold,
With such sweet cheer and countenance
As was at their love's severance ;
He calls to mind how she made oath
980 To him, at parting, of her troth,
Then weeps and for her pardon cries
For thinking in such foolish wise,
And knows full well he is deceived
By that mad anger which him grieved.
985 For this he carved that image well
That he thereto his heart would tell,
All his good thoughts and all his madness,

His pangs of love and his love's gladness,
Where else confide his story dire
990 Of body's will and heart's desire?

So Tristan suffers love's tormenting,
Oft fleeing thence, and oft relenting,
Kind talk with her doth often hold,
And oft unkind, as I have told.
995 Love unto this doth him constrain,
Filling his heart with error vain.
Had he not loved her utterly
He never had felt jealousy;
His doubts are caused by this alone,
1000 That he loves her, and save her, none.
For loved he any other where
He'd have no jealousy of her;
His jealousy doth thus abuse her
Only because he fears to lose her.
1005 No thought of loss would him affright
Were not his love of such great might;
For what a man doth lightly hold,
Its woe or welfare leaves him cold.
How should he be disquieted
1010 For what ne'er comes into his head?
Strange was the love betwixt these four,
And all great grief and dolour bore,
And each and all must live in woe,
Not one can any pleasure know.
1015 For first, King Mark is well assured
Iseult to him hath broken word
And loves another man much more;

He cannot help but grieve therefor.
This racks him with a torment grim,
1020   Anguish of heart it is to him,
For he loves nothing, nor desires,
Except Iseult that of him tires.
Though of her flesh he take his will,
Little content his heart can fill
1025   When her whole love is elsewhere given ;
Right wood and mad thereby he's driven ;
This is a perdurable dole,
That Tristan holds her heart and soul.
And next to him, Iseult must grieve
1030   To have the thing she fain would leave,
And, on the other hand, forgo
The thing for which she yearneth so.
One pain alone the king doth tear,
Iseult a double load must bear :
1035   Tristan she lacks, and is beside
Unto another husband tied ;
She may not quit him nor forsake,
And yet no joy in him can take.
She hath his body, spurns his heart,
1040   This torment first doth make her smart ;
Second, her love's on Tristan laid,
And Mark her husband hath forbade
That e'er the twain should meet again
Yet him she loves alone of men,
1045   And knows none liveth under sky
Whom Tristan loves so tenderly ;
Well loves she him, he loves her well,
He may not have her ; this is hell.

A double pain, a double woe
1050 Tristan for love must undergo :
Wedded to this Iseult, he still
Neither can love her nor yet will.
In law he may not quit her side,
In his despite must with her bide,
1055 Since she will never loose her grasp.
Little it likes him her to clasp,
Save that he findeth some small meed
Of comfort in her name, indeed.
That which he hath doth him annoy,
1060 And worse, that he may not enjoy
The queen his love on any wise,
To whom alone he lives and dies.
Thus two-fold strength the sorrow finds
Which Iseult's love on Tristan binds.
1065 For this love's sake, full sadly stands
His wife, Iseult of the White Hands :
However *that* Iseult may fare
This grieves in comfortless despair ;
She of her husband gets no mirth,
1070 And loves no other man on earth,
Hers she would have him, hers he is,
Yet can she gain no moment's bliss.
Mark is in better case than she,
Since he of Iseult's bed is free
1075 E'en though her heart escape his thrall,
But she can get no joy at all.

   .   .   .   .   .

Only love Tristan without joy.
Fain would she take with him her pleasure,

She gets but misery out of measure.
1080 When she most longs to clasp and kiss
And win him to love's ecstasies,
He still is bounden to withstand it
And she, for shame, will not demand it.
Now, then, I cannot still decide
1085 Which of these four was sorest tried,
Nor can I even to judge begin,
Being unproven quite herein.
I will but tell the story through;
But verdict is from lovers due,
1090 Whether of these four loved the best,
Or whose grief was the bitterest.

Dan Mark on Iseult's flesh hath power
To work his will at any hour,
Yet this torments him grievously,
1095 That Tristan is more loved than he,
Since he loves none but her alone.
And Iseult the king's sway must own
And yield her body to his will;
Often she weeps for this sore ill:
1100 She in the king takes no delight,
But bears this as a master's right;
Else all desire in her is cold
Save this: love Tristan to behold,
That is new wed in country strange;
1105 She fears his heart hath suffered change,
Though against hope she hopeth yet
His love is on none other set.
Tristan desires Iseult alone,

Yet knows that Mark her lord doth own
1110 And hold at will her body's treasure;
And he himself can get no pleasure,
Barred from desire and will likewise.
A wife he hath, yet neither lies
With her, nor loves her any jot;
1115 Yet 'gainst his heart he sinneth not.
Iseult of the White Hands, his wife,
Who asks no other thing of life
But Tristan, her dear lord, alone,
His body, not his heart, doth own,
1120 Lacks the one thing for which she burns.
Now let him say whom it concerns
Whose love was happiest of these four,
And which the bitterest sorrow bore.

Iseult, the fair, white-handed may,
1125 Beside her lord a virgin lay;
Together in one bed they lie:
What of their joy or grief know I?
He will not grant her that delight
Which is a married woman's right,
1130 But if she even knows of this,
Or if such life be grief or bliss,
I know not; surely, had she grieved,
She had not so long time deceived
Her friends with silence as she did.
1135 Now on a day it thus betid
That, called with all their neighbours round,
Tristan and Kaherdin went bound
At some high feast to make their prayer;

By Tristan's wish Iseult was there :
1140   Kaherdin on his right did ride,
Holding her bridle's left-hand side.
Thus with gay gossip forth they go,
And in their talk are busied so
They heed not how they ride, but still
1145   Let their steeds go their own sweet will—
Till suddenly Kaherdin's lunges
Against Iseult's, which rears and plunges.
She with the rowel smites him well,
And lightly rising from the selle
1150   To spur a second time his side,
Needs was her fair thigh lifted wide,
While she grips fast with her right knee.
Her horse leaps forward hastily,
And stumbles with his feet astray
1155   Into a little water-way,
His hoofs that day being newly shod ;
Splash in the slippery pool he trod ;
And as he flounders in the slough
He churns the pool about, till now
1160   Above her knee the water flies,
Spraying upon her parted thighs,
As still she sought to spur his side.
So, startled by the cold, she cried
Aloud ; and then was silent quite
1165   Save that she 'gan to laugh outright
With such loud mirth as nought could stay,
Were it at Mass on a Good Friday.
Kaherdin sees her laugh like this,
Thinks she has heard him speak amiss,

1170 And noted in him some absurd,
Discourteous or unseemly word—
For a right modest knight was he,
Amorous, frank, of good degree.
So, when his sister's mirth he hears,
1175 Some folly on his part he fears,
And to have said some shameful thing.
Therefore he falls a-questioning :
" Iseult, a hearty laugh that was,
But still I do not know the cause ;
1180 Show me, I pray, the reason plain,
Else will I trust you never again.
You make a mock of me no doubt ;
If I hereafter find it out,
I shall not feel such trust in you
1185 Nor love, as is to sisters due."
Iseult well hears him ask her this,
Knows he will take it much amiss,
Should she be silent, thus besought,
So says : " I laughed at my own thought—
1190 Of an adventure that fell out
Which I must laugh to think about.
This water that splashed up so high
Reached far more boldly to my thigh
Than hand of man e'er reached unto
1195 Or ever Tristan sought to do.
Now, brother, have I told thee why. . ."

The End of the First Turin Fragment.

Kaherdin promptly replied :
" What do you mean, Iseult ? Does not

Tristan treat you as a man should treat his lawful wife?"

"Never. I am still a clean maiden."

Then Kaherdin was angry. "Doubtless," said he, "Tristan takes his pleasure elsewhere. Had I known this, you should never have married him."

But Iseult said: "You have no right to accuse him. He has some other reason. I will hear nothing against him."

Kaherdin pondered much on this insult to his sister. He rode moodily at Tristan's side, without speaking. And from that day he was cold to his former friend.

At length Tristan asked him the reason for his altered behaviour. Kaherdin mastered his anger and reproached him courteously, saying:

"Tristan, my sister tells me that you do not treat her rightly as your wife. How have we deserved this insult? Iseult is noble, courteous, beautiful, virtuous and well-brought-up; and yet it seems you refuse to have a son of our race. Were we not such fast friends, you would have to answer for your conduct. Why did you wed her if you were unwilling to make her your wife?"

Tristan answered:

"You say your sister is noble, courteous, full of virtue, beauty and accomplishments; but I must tell you that I have a lady so fair, noble, praiseworthy, great and honourable that her very waiting-woman so surpasses your sister in beauty, nobility, grace and courtesy as to be more worthy to be a king's bride than your sister to be a baron's lady. I say no word in disparagement of your sister; she is all that is beautiful, noble and good. Judge therefore, how great is the worth and praise of her whom I love above all living women!"

Kaherdin answered angrily:

"Such things are easily said. Show me this incomparable lady; else will I never believe it."

Then said Tristan:

"I confess that I have acted unworthily towards you, and I will explain the whole matter; for I would not there should be the least shadow of enmity between us. If I tell you my secret; if I show you this beautiful woman; promise me, by the bond of our friendship, never to reveal the matter to your sister or to any other."

So Kaherdin gave Tristan his promise, and early one morning the two friends rode away together into the great forest, till they came to the river and the ford.

Then said Kaherdin:

"Tristan, hast thou brought me into a trap? If we cross this river, the giant will slay us."

But Tristan called to Moldagog, who came out, and at Tristan's command threw down his club. So they passed over and came to the cave.

Kaherdin was greatly astonished to see the image of the giant at the door; he trembled, and could scarcely believe that it was not alive. But they passed it by and came to the image of Iseult, from which breathed so ravishing an odour that it overcame the senses. And Tristan clasped the image in his arms, crying :

"Sweet love ! I am tormented day and night for thy love ! I have no will nor desire in my life save the will and the desire of thee."

Great was Kaherdin's amazement at the beauty of the images ; for he thought that they were living women. "Tristan," said he, "I pray thee, let me share in thy pleasure. Let me have the love of the waiting-maid, as thou hast the love of the queen."

Then said Tristan : "Confess first that this waiting-maid is fairer than thy sister Iseult."

Kaherdin said : "I admit that she is beautiful indeed. I pray thee, let me have her."

Then said Tristan : "Take her ; she is thine."

So Kaherdin advanced to the image of Brangwain, and sought to take the golden goblet from her hand. But when he found that he could not move it, he looked more closely and perceived that these were only images. In great anger he cried out :

"Thou hast deceived me, Tristan ! False art thou to faith and friendship if thou give me not the maiden herself according to thy promise !"

Tristan promised that he would do so. And he showed Kaherdin all the marvels of the cave.

And when they had returned to the castle, they gave out that they were about to go on pilgrimage. And taking with them only two attendants and arming themselves for the journey, they departed and took ship. . . .

Here begins the First Fragment of Strasburg.

And forth to England haste amain
To see Iseult, to seek Brangwain ;
Brangwain was sought by Kaherdin,
1200 But Tristan sought Iseult the Queen.

Why should I make so long a tale
To tell you things that nought avail ?
This is the sum and this the end :
Tristan and Kaherdin his friend
1205 So long together ride and go
They come a city's gates unto
Where Mark that night designs to lie.
So hearing that he must pass by,
Tristan, who well that roadway knows,
1210 With Kaherdin to meet him goes ;
Far down the way they ride, and see
The passing of the king's meinie,
And when the king's rout had gone past
They see the queen's train follow last.
1215 Then from the road they turn them straight
Leaving their servants to await,
And mount into an oak-tree high
That in a side-path grew near by,
Whence they the highway well may scan
1220 Themselves unseen of any man.
There go the boys, the pages go,
The brachets, and the hounds also,
Footmen and servants of the chase,
And kennel-men, and scullions base,
1225 There go the grooms and foragers,

The hunters and the destriers,
The palfreys and the sumpter-beasts,
And men with hawks upon their wrists.
There was a goodly meinie seen,
1230   And greatly marvels Kaherdin
To look upon so large a train
And the brave shows it doth contain,
And that so far he hath not seen
The fair maid Brangwain nor the queen.
1235   Lo ! now the lavenders arrayed,
And many a common chamber-maid
That did the general work for all—
Made beds, set tables up in hall,
Mended the linen, washed folks' hair,
1240   And did such other service there.
Kaherdin cries : " I see her now ! "
Said Tristan : " Faith, so dost not thou ;
These be her chamber-women, who
Her coarsest household labour do."
1245   Next, see ! the chamberlains ride past,
And now the press grows thicker fast
Of many a squire and many a knight,
Well-nurtured, courtly, fair to sight,
Singing sweet songs and pastourelles.
1250   And after go the damoiselles,
Daughters of lords and princes free
And sprung from many a far country ;
These pass with music and glad song ;
Their lovers ride with them along,
1255   Clerkly and valiant men they seem,
And love is evermore their theme,

Of true love and of ladies' glances
And of love's sweetest semblances
According as in love they find
1260   Right powerful cause to turn their mind
Towards them to whom they've sworn
        love's vow.*
Kaherdin cries : " I see her now !
There rides the queen, the first in train,
And where is now the maid Brangwain ? "

The End of the First Fragment of Strasburg.

But at length, after Kaherdin had many times
been mistaken, Iseult and Brangwain came by,
riding together in the same litter. Kaherdin was
amazed. He could not choose but admit that
Queen Iseult was the loveliest of all women born,
and that even Brangwain far excelled in beauty
his own sister, Iseult of the White Hands.

Now it fell out that a halt was made in the royal
progress, close beside the tree in which the friends
were hidden. Tristan therefore slipped on to
Kaherdin's finger the ring which Iseult had given
to him and bade him go forward and contrive in
some way to show it to Iseult. So Kaherdin
climbed down and approached the queen's litter,
and courteously asked the road to the nearest inn,
as though he were a traveller that had lost his way.
In the litter, close beside the queen, was the dog
Petit-crû in his beautiful kennel, and while Kaherdin was talking, and while Brangwain was looking

* Vv. 1257-1261 : fragmentary in the original and conjecturally
restored in translation.

on him with favour, he caressed Petit-crû, stroking
him so insistently and so often that Iseult noticed
the ring upon his hand and understood that he was
a messenger from Tristan. She said therefore :

"Pass on quickly ; delay us no longer. I feel
myself unwell, and am anxious to reach yonder
castle, where I shall lie to-night."

When Kaherdin brought back this report,
Tristan understood that Iseult had seen the ring and
sought to tell them what road they should take.

The king and his company came to the castle
and prepared their lodging for the night. After
supper, the queen feigned sickness. She retired
to a separate lodging within the castle grounds,
taking with her only Brangwain and a young
serving-maid. When they had all gone to rest,
Tristan and Kaherdin left their squires to guard
the horses and the arms, and went secretly to the
queen's lodging. There he and the queen met
and embraced each other with joy ; and Tristan
presented Kaherdin to the queen and to Brangwain. And while Tristan and Iseult talked joyously
together, Kaherdin paid court to Brangwain.

Presently, they went to bed. Tristan lay with
the queen, and Kaherdin took Brangwain within
his arms. But Brangwain had a little silken
cushion, curiously embroidered ; and when she
put it under Kaherdin's head, he fell into a deep
slumber and woke no more till late the following
morning. He gazed about him and knew not
where he was ; but when he saw that Brangwain

had already risen, and that they were all laughing at him, he understood that he had been cheated by some enchantment.

On the next night, the same thing happened again. But the third night, Iseult took pity on Kaherdin and besought Brangwain that she should no longer use him so ill. She told her how brave and courteous a knight Kaherdin was, and that it would be a great honour to have him for a lover. So Brangwain gave way and submitted gladly to Kaherdin's love; and they passed their time in great joyousness all four together.

Presently, however, it came about that their secret was discovered and they were forced to part. Tristan and Kaherdin, being warned in time, made their escape; but they could not, for the time being, get back to the place where they had left their horses and armour.

But Cariado, who was seeking Tristan everywhere, came first upon the horses. And the squires, who saw him coming, leapt quickly into the saddle and galloped away, taking with them the arms and shields of their masters. Cariado thought they were Tristan and Kaherdin in person, and rode after them, crying out:

" Hold! hold! Return and do battle for your lives! Shame upon you, coward knights! What? do you flee for fear of death? Have you not come from the arms of your ladies? Your flight does them foul dishonour! "

So said Cariado. But the squires rode so fast

that he could not overtake them. So presently
he returned to the castle. There he found Brangwain, and mocked her with bitter words.

"A right cowardly knight hast thou taken for
thy lover!" said he. "This is indeed honourable—to have to do with a gallant who flees
from an armed man like a hare before the hounds!
Again and again I summoned him to turn and
fight, and he was so afeard he would not so much
as look round! Worthily hast thou done to
give thy love to the most recreant knight alive!
But thou wast ever a foolish wench!"

When Brangwain heard these insults . . . .

*Here begins the Last Part of the Poem, which is put
together from the Douce Fragment (the 1268th
to the 3087th line), the Second Turin Fragment (the
1265th to the 1518th line), the Second Strasburg
Fragment (the 1489th to the 1493rd and the 1615th
to the 1688th line), the Third Strasburg Fragment
(the 1785th to the 1854th line), and the Second
Sneyd Fragment (the 2319th to the 3144th line).*

1265   Right woe she is and wroth at heart ;
        Angrily doth she thence depart
        And seeketh out Iseult alone
        Where she for Tristan maketh moan.
        "Lady," quoth Brangwain, "woe is me !
1270   Woe worth the hour I looked on thee—
        On thee, and Tristan thy sweet make !
        I left my country for thy sake,
        And then, to make thy folly good,
        Lady, I lost my maidenhood,

1275   Certes, 'twas done for love of thee ;
        Honour enough ye promised me,
        Thou and Tristan the perjurèd—
        May all ill-hap light on his head,
        Cumber his life and bring to blame !
1280   Through him was I first put to shame.
        Remember where you sent me then,
        And gave command I should be slain ;
        Small thanks to your good grace, I wot,
        That your serfs spared, and slew me not ;
1285   I of their hatred gat more good
        Than of thy friendship, Queen Isoud.
        Foolish was I and weak of wit
        Since then to trust thee any whit,
        Or ever bear thee love and faith
1290   Since hearing that decree of death.
        Why sought I not the death of thee
        Who soughtst it thus for guiltless me ?
        I pardoned all that former crime,
        But 'tis renewed a second time
1295   By the ill trap you took me in
        Treacherously with Kaherdin.
        Curse upon your good grace, I say,
        If thus my service you repay !
        Prithee, is this the honour vast
1300   You give for all my love that's past ?
        Methinks he sought a bed-fellow
        Only his cowardice to show,
        Yea, and you urged him on to this
        To drag me into foolishness ;
1305   Lady, you've put on me this slight

> To glut your own malicious spite.
> Wholly dishonoured now I prove—
> This is the end of all our love.
> God ! how you praised him day by day
> 1310 To lead me on into love's way—
> Never was man of his degree,
> His prowess, praise and bravery ;
> Eh ! what a knight you made him out,
> In all the world was none so stout—
> 1315 Who is the coward most abhorred
> That e'er set hand to shield or sword !
> He that from Cariado flees
> Ruin and shame his body seize !
> Who flees before so poor a knight
> 1320 'Twixt here and Rome's no worser wight.
> Come, tell me now, Iseult the queen,
> How long time you a bawd have been ?*
> Where did you learn the trade so well
> Of evil men such good to tell,
> 1325 And cheat a wretched woman so ?
> Why must you bring me down so low
> For the worst man the world has bred ?
> So many brave men sought my bed ;—
> I could defend me 'gainst them all,
> 1330 And now must to a coward fall !
> And all was by your urging on—

---

* Literally : Tell me now, therefore, Queen Iseult,
          How long have you become Richeult ?

The name " Richeult " is used as the type of a bawd, as who
should say " Pandar."   A poem of 1159, entitled " De Richeut "
alludes to earlier tales dealing with the adventures of this famous
personage.

Whereof I'll be revenged anon,
On you and Tristan by my oath ;
I bid defiance to you both ;
1335   Ill will I work to you and blame
For the deep vileness of my shame."

When Iseult hears this angry pride,
And when she hears herself defied
By her whom most of all she must
1340   Believe, and with her honour trust,
(For she to her is lief and dear
That now so foully rateth her),
She's struck with anguish to the heart
To hear such wrath against her start ;
1345   Straight to her heart the anger goes,
Her heart is wrung by double woes,
She knows not what defence to make
Nor which she first shall undertake ;
She sighs and says : " Ah, wretched ! O !
1350   Why was I not dead long ago ?
Nought but ill fortune comes to hand
Here in this luckless foreign land.
Tristan, a curse upon you lie !
You brought me to this misery,
1355   You to this shore fetched me away
Where I'm in torment every day.
For you my lord doth hate me so,
And no man here but is my foe
By open hate or secret guile.
1360   What then ?   I bore it a long while,
And could have borne it to the end

H

If only Brangwain were my friend.
But if she turn against me too
And hate me—why, what can I do ?
1365 She that my only comfort was
Will shame me, Tristan, thou being cause.
Ill was the hour I first loved thee,
Such wrath, such hate is fall'n on me !
You've robbed me of my kinsmen, and
1370 Of all men's love in this strange land,
Yet these things seem to you but small
Till you have robbed me last of all
Of such sole comfort as was left ;
I must of Brangwain be bereft.
1375 More noble, valiant, loyal more
Was never damozel before ;
You and Kaherdin, traitors twain,
Subtly have stol'n away Brangwain,
You need her in your distant land
1380 To guard Iseult of the White Hand ;
Because you know her true and tried
She shall keep watch upon your bride.
Your treacherous way to me you wend
To steal away my childhood's friend.
1385 O Brangwain, think upon my sire,
My mother's prayer, and fond desire !
If thou desert me in this plight,
In this strange country, friendless quite,
What shall I do ?   How can I live ?
1390 No one can any comfort give.
Nay, Brangwain, if thou'rt bent to leave me
Thou needst not thus with hatred grieve me.

Nor on a trumped-up quarrel lay
The blame for journeying far away.
1395 Gladly I give good leave to thee,
If thou with Kaherdin wouldst be ;
I know 'tis Tristan makes thee do
This thing—which God send he may rue ! ”

When she had heard Iseult, Brangwain
1400 From harsh reply cannot refrain,
Says : “ Evil is your heart, I trow,
To speak such wild words of me now,
Things that I never dreamed nor thought.
Pray you, what ill has Tristan wrought ?
1405 On you should light the shame, who still
Delight to practise it at will.
Were all your heart not set on wrong
You would not practise it thus long.
The evil lust that in you burns
1410 Haply to-day on Tristan turns,
Though had there never been Tristan
Your love had been for some worse man.
I've no complaint against his love,
But bitter thoughts my grief doth move
1415 'Gainst you, that plotted my distress
Just to indulge your wickedness.
I am dishonoured quite if e'er
I help you more.   Henceforth beware !
I will have vengeance if I can !
1420 If you must mate me to a man
Could you not find one, if you would,
That had some touch of knightlihood,

Not snare me, in your treacherous scorn,
With the most coward villain born ? "

1425 " Mercy, sweet friend," Iseult replies,
" I never harmed you in no wise,
Neither for hurt nor malice was
This plan contrived and brought to pass ;
I sought to do the best for thee,
1430 Guiltless, God knows, of treachery.
Kaherdin is a knight of pride,
A rich duke and a warrior tried,
Never believe that he for dread
Of Cariado could have fled ;
1435 Rather they tell this tale for spite,
Since sure he ne'er from him took flight.
Though you should hear him slandered sore,
You must not hate him thus therefore,
Nor Tristan my dear love, nor me.
1440 Brangwain, I swear that verily,
Howe'er this matter may befal,
They of this court are plotters all,
And purposed to embroil us twain,
Whereof our foes would be right fain.
1445 Think, who will seek my honour now
If thou shouldst hate me, Brangwain, thou ?
How shall I ever honoured be
If I dishonoured am by thee ?
None can by treason so offend
1450 As one's own close familiar friend,
The friend that all one's secrets knows,
Turning to hate, can all disclose ;

And thou that of my counsel art
Canst shame me, if thou hast the heart.

1455 But foul reproach it were that thou
Which wast my counsellor till now,
Brangwain, shouldst let thy wrath have
    sway
And to the king my trust betray.
On other wise I did for you ;

1460 Wrong must not be betwixt us two.
Truly, this quarrel is but nought ;
You know, your shame I never sought,
Only your honour and great good.
Ah ! put away this angry mood.

1465 How will you profit anything
Though I be ruined with the king ?
Surely my ruin and mischance
In nothing will your cause advance ;
Nay, if you bring me to disgrace

1470 You'll have the less of love and praise.
By some indeed you'll be approved
By whom 'tis shameful to be loved,
But you will be the more despised
By courteous men and well-advised.

1475 And all my love will be the cost,
And my lord's friendship will be lost.
Whatever face he turn on me
Never believe he'll not hate thee.
His love for me is so right great,

1480 No man could turn it into hate ;
No man could make such mischief ever
As my lord's love from me to sever ;

Howe'er my conduct cause him pain
He'll strive to hate me—all in vain !
1485 Though for my folly he must grieve,
He knows no way my love to leave ;
He hates my sin, yet, 'gainst his will,
Try as he may, he'll love me still.
None that e'er sought me to decry
1490 Unto the king, gat good thereby.
Think you he would not hate them sore
That these most hateful tidings bore ?
What profit were it to the king
To hear of me this shameful thing ?
1495 What vengeance have you helped him to,
Though me you wholly should undo ?
What will this treachery avail ?
You'll go to him with what new tale ?
That Tristan came and talked with me ?
1500 Well, and thereby what harm has he ?
And tell me what he stands to gain
If you put wrath betwixt us twain ?
He is no way the worse for this."
Brangwain replies : " A year it is
1505 Since he forbade, and you forswore
To love or speak with Tristan more.
The king's forbidding and your oath,
Foully have you observed them both ;
Soon as thou hadst the power—O scorn !
1510 Wretched Iseult, thou wast forsworn,
False to thy faith and perjurèd.
So 'prenticed to the devil's trade
Thou art, thou never canst refrain,

Still must thou hug the same old chain.
1515 Sin must have been thy childhood's play,
So to sin on from day to day ;
Didst thou not take delight in wrong
Thou hadst not held to sin so long ;
A colt's first lesson with the rein,
1520 Will he or nill he, he'll retain,
And what a woman learns in youth,
Save it be beaten out, in truth
All her life long bides with her still,
So she have power to serve her will.
1525 You in your childhood learned that same,
And all your life 'twill be your aim ;
If in your youth 'twere not your learning,
You would not still thereto be turning,
Or had the king chastisèd you
1530 You would not seek this ill to do ;
But just because he'll pass this o'er,
You go on sinning more and more.
Now for this cause he passed it by,
That he had no full certainty ;
1535 Now shall he have the truth, I say,
And then do with it as he may.
You've made such custom of love's play
You've flung your honour all away,
So closely you to folly cleave,
1540 It will not leave you till life leave ;
When first in this the king surprised you
He ought by right to have chastised you,
But he has suffered it so long,
He's made a mock to all the throng.

1545 He should have cut your nose away,
     Or branded you some other way,
     Till your whole life was one disgrace,
     And you the shame of all your race.
     Surely, 'twere well you should have shame
1550 That on your friends, upon your name,
     Upon your lord, this shame have brought.
     Had you of honour any thought
     You'ld seek this evil forth to thrust.
     Well do I know wherein you trust:
1555 The lustful weakness of the king!
     From you he'll suffer any thing;
     Because to hate you he's no power
     You shame him every day and hour;
     Because his love for you's so strong
1560 He'll suffer any shame and wrong.
     Surely, had he not loved you so,
     He had chastised you long ago.
     Nor will I spare, but say to you.
     This is a wicked thing you do,
1565 And in your flesh an evil smutch,
     That this man should love you so much,
     While unto him, yourself you bear
     As you did less than nothing care;
     If in your heart he'd any place
1570 You would not compass his disgrace."

     When Queen Iseult these insults hears,
     Wrathful she speaks to Brangwain's ears:
     " You judge me far too cruelly,
     Cursèd of God your judgment be !

1575 Thou speakst as one devoid of grace
When me thou callest treachour base !
Certes, if I be so forsworn,
So perjured, false and put to scorn,
So much a thing of sin and stain,
1580 Who counselled me but you, Brangwain ?
Had it not been by your consent
We ne'er had been on madness bent ;
By your consent did this begin,
'Twas you that taught me how to sin,
1585 All our great schemes, the bitter smart,
The doubts, and all the grief of heart,
And all the love betwixt us two—
If this was wrought, 'twas wrought through
    you.
Traitor to me at first thou wast,
1590 To Tristan next, to King Mark last ;
Long had he known the truth of this
But for thy subtle trickeries.
The lies you told him day by day,
They kept us in the evil way ;
1595 By cunning sleights and by deceits
You covered up our evil feats.
You more than I have been to blame
Because you thrust me into shame
Who once was placed beneath your care.
1600 Now you will lay the story bare
Of how, when in your care, I fell.
God smite me with the fire of hell
If, once this truth be brought to day,
I hide one single thing away !

1605 If Mark avenge himself at all
On you first shall his vengeance fall !
You at his hand deserve no less.
Yet, I cry mercy ne'ertheless,
Pray you to let my secret be
1610 And turn away your wrath from me."
Brangwain replies : " Not I, in sooth !
First shall the king know all the truth ;
Who's right, who wrong, we then shall know,
And, as it may be, be it so ! "
1615 She leaves Iseult in wrath of soul,
Swearing, the king shall learn the whole.

Forth to the king in anger goes
Brangwain, to tell him all she knows ;
" Hear me, Messire," she says, " and heed
1620 All I shall say as truth indeed."
Yet with feigned words weaves all the while
A cunning web, wrought out with guile.
She says " A little list to me :
I owe you faith and fealty,
1625 And truth and stedfast love I owe
Your honour, and yourself also ;
If I see aught that works you shame
I ought, methinks, to give it name ;
Had this been earlier known to me
1630 I should have told you instantly.
But this I must of Iseult say,
She gets more wicked every day ;
Her heart to sin grows more attached,
And if she be not better watched

1635 She of her body will do ill,
      Whereof, till now, she's guiltless still,
      Yet waits but opportunity.
      Your doubts all misdirected lie:
      Which much bewilders me, and frets,
1640 And doubt and fear within me sets,
      For she will stick at nothing, till,
      By hook or crook she have her will.
      I come to counsel you therefore
      To have her watched and guarded more.
1645 Have you ne'er heard, then, in your life:
      ' An empty bed makes a foolish wife,
      Easy of access makes the thief,
      A foolish wife brings the house to grief?'
      You were at fault some time agone,
1650 Nor was mine own mind clear thereon,
      Though I kept watch by morn and eve.
      Yet it was useless, I believe,
      She has deceived us all along,
      Our thoughts, our doubts, have all been
          wrong,
1655 She's tricked us by a sly device,
      And, without casting, changed the dice;
      Now let us trick her ere she cast,
      Lest she attain her end at last,
      And carry thus her purpose through
1660 As surely 'tis her will to do:
      If for a little we restrain her,
      After, I think, she will refrain her.
      This is your duty, Mark, I swear,
      Certes a shameful thing it were

1665 Still to condone her sin—let bide
Her leman ever at her side.
Foolish I am, I know that well,
A single word of this to tell,
You'll bear a grudge for all my pains.
1670 There, anyhow, the truth remains.
But, though you hide your thoughts, I wis,
Whatever face you put on this,
That you will never have the heart
Courageously to do your part.
1675 Seeing how much you knew before,
Sir King, 'twere needless to say more."

The king gives ear to Brangwain's word,
And marvels much at what he's heard,
Wonders what all this tale's about
1680 Of his dishonour and his doubt,
His suffering that and knowing this,
What thoughts he hides, what face is his.
Wholly bewildered is his state:
He begs her speak the truth out straight,
1685 Tristan, he thinks, must be once more
In the queen's chamber as before.
He gives his word, with promise leal,
He'll counsel keep and nought reveal.
Brangwain continues cunningly:
1690 " King, though I lose my charge thereby,
The queen's intrigue I will not hide,
Nor the love-bond which she has tied.
We have been all this time deceived
In what we falsely have believed,

1695   That she to Tristan was giv'n o'er :
      She has a nobler servitor,
      Count Cariado is his name ;
      He is about her to your shame ;
      So long of love he her requires
1700   Methinks she'll grant what he desires ;
      Through courtship long he's gained such
          power
      She'll take him to her paramour.
      Yet has he had no more, I vow,
      Of Iseult than of me, till now ;
1705   He might have done—I could not say—
      Had the occasion come their way.
      Wily he is and fair to sight,
      And he's about her day and night,
      Pleading and flattering and praising.
1710   If she do folly, is't amazing,
      With a fine man, so amorous ?
      But *you* amaze me, sire, that thus
      Let him about her come and go.
      What is it makes you love her so ?
1715   Tristan's the only man you fear,
      But now it is to me quite clear
      That love for him she has no whit,
      For she, too, was deceived in it.
      When last he came to England's shore
1720   Your peace and favour to implore,
      So soon as Iseult heard it, she
      Sent Cariado privily
      To lie in wait for him and slay—
      Who chased him forth and far away.

1725   I know not rightly what did hap,
       But it was Iseult set the trap,
       And sure she'd not cause shame to fall
       On any man she loved at all.
       If he be slain, great sin it were,
1730   He's courteous, brave and debonair,
       And nephew, sire, to you by blood ;
       You'll never find a friend as good."
       When Mark the king had heard this tale
       His heart did in his body fail,
1735   He knows not what is to be done,
       And will no further speak thereon,
       Not seeing aught hereby to gain ;
       He saith in private to Brangwain :
       " I promise faithfully, my friend,
1740   'Gainst you I nothing will intend,
       Only, to best of my endeavour
       Cariado from the court I'll sever.
       I place Iseult beneath your charge ;
       Suffer her not to talk at large
1745   With knight or noble privily
       Save you be of the company ;
       She's in your care, for word and deed—
       From this day forth 'tis thus agreed."
       Now is Iseult beneath the hand
1750   Of Brangwain, and in her command,
       May nought in private say or do
       Without Brangwain be present too.
       Tristan and Kaherdin depart
       Upon their way, right sad at heart.
1755   Iseult is left in sorrow deep,

And Brangwain her own wrongs doth weep.
Mark, too, is filled with grief of soul,
And for his error makes great dole.
And Cariado's sad enough :
1760   Ceaseless he strives for Iseult's love,
Yet whatsoever he may try
Always she will her love deny ;
Yet he to Mark betrayeth nought.
Now then it comes to Tristan's thought
1765   That he dishonoured home returns
Save both the what and why he learns
Of how the world with Iseult goes,
And what the noble Brangwain does.
He Kaherdin to God commends
1770   And all the long road backward wends,
Swearing he never can be glad
Till he some news of them has had.
Right fast is Tristan in love's thrall ;
Vile rags he clothes himself withal,
1775   With wretched rags, a beggar's dress,
So that no man nor maid might guess
That this is Tristan the good knight.
He's by a herb disguisèd quite,
Which doth his visage puff and change,
1780   As swollen by disease, and strange ;
And, scrutiny still more to cheat,
He crooks his hands and twists his feet,
And wraps him in a leper's hood,
Then takes in hand a bowl of wood,
1785   Which in their love's first year had been
A gift unto him from the queen,

Therein he sets a boxwood stake,
A leper's rattle for to make.
Then to the court he hies him straight,
1790   And lingers long by every gate ;
Much he desires to know and see
How all things at the court may be.
Oft begs, oft sounds his rattle clear,
But still he can no tidings hear
1795   Whereby his joy may be increased.
One day the king was holding feast,
And to the minster forth did pass
There to attend a great High Mass.
He rides forth from his palace high,
1800   And after him the queen rides by.
Tristan beholds—for alms he pleads,
But she nor knows him nor yet heeds ;
He runs behind, his rattle chimes,
Calls on her name a hundred times,
1805   Beseeches alms for God's dear sake,
Piteous and sad lament doth make.
Uproarious is the mirth, I ween,
Among the men that guard the queen.
He's seized, he's tumbled in the dust,
1810   And rudely from the rout is thrust,
One threatens him, another beats.
Still he clings on, and still repeats
In God's own name, his prayer for aid ;
For no threats will he be afraid.
1815   They think him troublesome indeed,
Nor know how instant is his need.
He to the chapel follows close,

Beating his bowl with sounding blows.
Iseult at length is wholly vexed,
1820   Stares at him angry and perplexed,
She cannot think what's in his mind
That he thus follows close behind.
Sudden the well-known cup she spied
And knew 'twas Tristan at her side,
1825   By his fair form and by his stature,
And by his body's shape and nature.
A terror to her heart doth smite,
And all her face grows wan and white,
For very much she fears the king.
1830   She draweth off a golden ring,
But knows not how she shall bestow it.
Into his bowl she seeks to throw it,
But as in hand she holds it high,
Brangwain espies her suddenly,
1835   Then looks on Tristan—on the spot
She knows him and sees through the plot.
Madman and fool she calls him then
So to thrust in 'mongst noble men,
The guards, she cries, are villains found
1840   To suffer him amongst the sound ;
For her deceit she scolds the queen :
" Since when have you so saintly been
That you must give so great largesse
To folk in sickness or distress ?
1845   You would bestow on him your ring ?
'Faith, madam, you'll do no such thing.
On such a scale you shall not give,
Or you'll repent it while you live,

And if you give it now away
1850   You shall repent this very day!"
She bids the soldiers round about
Forth of the church to put him out;
Therefore they thrust him from the door
And Tristan dare entreat no more.

1855   Tristan now sees, and sees full clear,
That Brangwain hates both him and her,
Therefore he knows not what to do,
His heart with grief is stricken through;
She's cast him out in vilest wise,
1860   And he laments with weeping eyes
His youth, and the mischance thereof,
That e'er he staked his all on love.
So many griefs did he sustain,
So many terrors, so much pain,
1865   So many hardships, so much danger,
So many times driv'n forth a stranger,
He cannot choose but sorrow for 't.
An ancient house stood in the court,
Decay'd, and fall'n to disrepair.
1870   He goes and crouches 'neath the stair,
Lamenting all his pain and woe—
How wearily his life doth go,
For he is all by travail worn,
Fasting and watching night and morn.
1875   With griefs and labours like to die,
Tristan beneath the stair doth lie,
Death must he seek and life despise,
Thence without help he'll never rise.

Iseult bemoans her wretched fate
1880 Most doleful and unfortunate,
Thus to behold in such sad plight
All she most loves beneath the light.
What's to be done she cannot see,
She weeps and sighs continually,
1885 Cursing each hour of every day
She in the living world doth stay.

They in the minster hear the Mass,
And after to the palace pass,
To keep their feast, and all the day
1890 In mirth and revel wears away ;
But for Iseult is no delight.
Now it fell out that ere the night
The porter found himself grow chill
Sitting within the gatehouse still ;
1895 Wherefore he doth his wife require
To fetch him wood to make a fire.
To go far out she did not care,
Bethought her that beneath the stair
Planks and dry wood were stowed away.
1900 Thither she runs without delay,
And in the darkness in doth creep ;
So comes on Tristan laid asleep,
Trips o'er his cloak, all hairy-lined.
She shrieks—she's half out of her mind,
1905 And, since she cannot make it out
Thinks 'tis the fiend, without a doubt ;
For deadly fear her heart doth quail
She flies to 'r husband with the tale.

He to the ruined house goes out
1910 And strikes a light and gropes about,
And there beholds Sir Tristan lie,
That is already near to die.
He wonders what this shape may be
And brings the candle close to see,
1915 And soon perceiveth, by its feature,
The thing's indeed a human creature,
But cold as ice in every limb.
Who is he ? he demands of him,
And whence ?   What makes he 'neath the
    stair ?
1920 Then Tristan lays the whole truth bare,
His state and station, and the case
That brings him to that dismal place.
Tristan much trusted this same man,
Who for his part, much loved Tristan,
1925 So with great toil and pain no lack
He bears him to his lodging back,
Lays him on pillow soft and good
And serves him well with wine and food.
Then to Iseult the word he bore,
1930 And to Brangwain as oft of yore,
But for no word that he could say
Would Brangwain any grace display.

Iseult calls Brangwain to her side :
" Ha, noble damozel ! " she cried,
1935 " Pity for Tristan I beseech—
I pray you go, with him have speech ;
Comfort him in his stark distress ;

He dies for grief and weariness ;
Such love of old you did him bear—
1940   Ah, comfort him, Brangwain the Fair !
Nought does he seek save you alone.
Go to him, and at least make known
Why and since when you're not his friend."
Brangwain replies : " All's to no end.
1945   By me he'll not be comforted.
I would more lief that he were dead
Than that he were alive and well.
Never again shall any tell
That you committed sin through me ;
1950   I will not cloke this villainy !
That was a vile thing that you said,
That you did all things by my aid,
And that by foul deceit I hid
All the misfeasance that you did.
1955   This comes of serving evil men ;
Sooner or late we lose our pain.
With all my power I served you still
And have gained nothing but ill-will.
Had you but thought what I deserved,
1960   Another way had I been served,
And got more guerdon for my toil
Than to be made a coward's spoil."
Iseult replies : " Ah, let that be !
Why must you still cast up at me
1965   The hasty words I once let fall ?
I am so sorry for it all.
I do beseech you, pardon me,   •
And go to Tristan speedily,

For he will ne'er be glad again
1970 Till he have spoken with Brangwain."
She coaxes her with such fair speeches
So wins, prays, promises, beseeches,
That she at length to Tristan hies
To bring him comfort where he lies.
1975 She finds the sick man very weak,
Feeble of body, pale of cheek,
Thin of his flesh and wan of blee.
She sees him weeping grievously,
And how full tenderly he sighs,
1980 And her entreats in piteous wise
Now for God's love, to let him know
What cause she has to hate him so,
For God's dear sake, to tell the truth.
Then, Tristan swears to her in sooth
1985 That she in this has been abused
Whereof Kaherdin stands accused,
Who shall return, and presently
Make Cariado eat his lie.
Brangwain believes him, takes his word,
1990 Soon they are once more in accord.
Together then the queen they sought
In chamber all of marble wrought,
Where in great love accorded, they
Comfort each other's grief away.
1995 Tristan of Iseult takes delight.
And after a great space of night
He takes farewell at break of day,
And to his own land turns away ;
He joins his brother's company,

2000 And with the first wind sails the sea
  Homeward to Iseult of Bretayn,
  Whom all this work puts much in pain.
  She's eaten up with jealous love,
  His heart is pierced with grief thereof,
2005 He feels great sorrow and great woe,
  Wondering his whole sad journey through,
  How can he love Iseult the White ?—
  This is his grief by day and night.

  So Tristan goes ; Iseult remains,
2010 And still for Tristan's love complains
  Because in evil case he goes ;
  But little of his state she knows.
  Now for the great woes' sake he bare,
  Which he in secret told to her,
2015 For all the pain, for all the ache
  Of love he suffered for her sake,
  For all the pang and all the smart,
  She in his penance will bear part ;
  Because she now sees Tristan languish
2020 She'd be his partner in the anguish ;
  Part in love's joy with him she had
  Who for love's sake is now so sad,
  And will with him take part likewise
  In all these woes and miseries.
2025 For her he suffers many a care
  Right grievous to his body fair,
  And in great grief his days doth spend ;
  And she that is the faithful friend
  Of all his thoughts, of all his need,

2030 Able his very heart to read,
Girds on (what love so faithful e'er ?)
To her nak'd flesh a shirt of hair,
Nor night nor day she lays it by
Save when she with the king doth lie ;
2035 And no man knew that this was so.
And she made oath and vow also
Never to put it off again
Till news of Tristan she should gain.
Right bitter penance, bitter passion,
2040 She bears for love in diverse fashion ;
For Tristan's sake a heavy dole
This Iseult bears in flesh and soul,
Discomfort and distress and pain.
One day she hath a fiddler ta'en
2045 And told him all the life she leads,
And all her case, and straitly pleads
That he will bear this word away
To him, and her whole mind convey.

When Tristan now this news doth hear
2050 Of her that is to him so dear,
He is cast down and in deep grief,
His heart can nowise find relief
Till he that shirt of hair have seen,
Girt, for his sake, about the queen ;
2055 It will not quit her tender flesh
Till to her land he come afresh.
He talks of this with Kaherdin,
Once more their journeyings begin ;
To England they return forthright

2060 To win adventure and delight,
  A pilgrim's semblance they've devised,
  Their faces stained, their dress disguised
  That no one may their secret know.
  To the king's court they straightway go,
2065 And there much private speech they use
  And take such pleasure as they choose.

  Once on a day the king held court,
  Thereunto did much folk resort;
  And after dinner they go play,
2070 And many a merry game essay
  Of wrestling and of sword-playing;
  And o'er them all was Tristan king.
  And next at the Welsh leap they vie,
  And then the leap of Galway try;
2075 The lists for jousting are set out,
  With darts they hold a contest stout,
  To spear and javelin they fall;
  Tristan wins more praise than they all;
  Kaherdin next in place did stand
2080 That conquered all by sleight of hand.
  And here was Tristan recognised
  And by a former friend surprised;
  Two steeds he gave into their hand,
  There were none better in the land,
2085 For he was set in great dismay
  Lest they should taken be that day,
  They put them in great hazard then—
  They slew outright two noble men,
  One, Cariado, the fair knight,

2090   Him Kaherdin o'erthrew in fight
       For that ill story which he spread,
       How he at their last meeting fled ;
       Thus was redeemed the solemn word
       He put in pledge at their accord.
2095   Then swiftly from that place they flee,
       To save their lives from jeopardy.

       Swift the companions spur away
       And to the sea-board make their way.
       There are they chased by Cornish folk,
2100   But they right quickly from them broke,
       Into the way of the woods wide
       Did Kaherdin and Tristan ride,
       And, wandering through the desert lands,
       On this wise kept them from their hands.
2105   Thus Brittany they lightly gain,
       And of their vengeance are full fain.

       Lords, here be many tales diverse
       Which I unite in this my verse,
       I tell the tale that seems the best,
2110   And simply put aside the rest,
       Nor, since the conflict here is such,
       Attempt to reconcile too much.
       For among those that sang of old
       And this fair tale of Tristan told
2115   Here there is great discrepancy.
       Many have told the tale to me,
       I know each story that they tell
       And everything they wrote as well,
       But yet, to judge from all I've heard,

2120 Many depart from Breri's word,
Who knew the gestes and chroniclings
Of all the courts and all the kings
That lived of old in Brittany.
Many beside this book there be
2125 That will not grant (what some folk tell)
How Kaherdin to loving fell
Of a dwarf's wife ; and how, in spite,
The jealous dwarf did Tristan smite,
With venomed spear, a treacherous blow,
2130 When Kaherdin he had laid low.
How Tristan, sick and stricken sore,
Sent Governal to England o'er,
Seeking Iseult to make him hale.
Thomas cannot admit this tale ;
2135 And therefore would by reason show
That surely it could not be so,
For it was known both far and wide
To all men in the country-side
That he in Tristan's cause did move,
2140 Messenger to Iseult of love.
Greatly therefore did Mark him hate,
Set men for him to lie in wait ;
How then could he have come to court
And there some kind of service sought
2145 With king or lord or soldiery,
Disguised as merchant from o'ersea ?
A man so known for miles about
Must very soon have been found out.
How should he guard his life and limb,
2150 And how bring Iseult back with him ?

Far from the tale these writers stray
And wander from the truth away.
If they to this will not consent
I'll make no further argument,
2155   Hold they to their tale, I to mine—
Truth shall prevail and brightly shine.

Tristan and Kaherdin depart
To Brittany, right glad at heart,
And joyously the days they spend
2160   With many a follower and friend.
They hunt the woods and countryside
Through all their marches tourneying ride,
Win praise and prizes by their hand
Before all others in the land
2165   For honour and for knightliness;
Or, when they sojourned in idlesse,
Into the bosky glade they went,
On those fair images intent;
For by those shapes their souls were moved
2170   Toward the fair women whom they loved:
And there by day they had delight
For all the anguish of the night.
Now on a day they hunting come
To fall of eve, so turn them home,
2175   All their companions they've outrun,
No man is there, save they alone.
So riding over the White Launde
They saw the sea at their right hand,
And how a knight to them made speed
2180   Galloping on a shining steed.

A right rich harness did he wear,
A golden shield, fretty of vair,
And such the colours of the lance,
The pennon and the cognisance.
2185 He rode a-gallop through the field
Crouched and close covered by his shield,
And he was full, and fair and tall,
A well-armed goodly knight withal.
And Tristan and Kaherdin bode
2190 Stoutly his coming in the road,
Marvelling much who this might be.
And straight unto the twain came he,
And in right courteous wise did greet;
Tristan returned him answer meet,
2195 Asking him whither, through the waste,
And to what end, he rode in haste.
" Pray you, fair sir," the knight replied,
" Know you the castle where doth bide
Tristan, whom men the Lover name ? "
2200 " Yea, and what would you with that same ? "
Said Tristan, " and what name have you ?
We'll bring you Tristan's house unto,
But if you would with Tristan speak
You need not any further seek,
2205 For I am Tristan verily ;
Tell me what you would have of me."
" Good news," quoth he, " and fair befall !
Tristan the Dwarf do men me call,
Born in the Marches of Bretayn,
2210 I dwell beside the Sea of Spain.
There in my house I had a fere

That more than life to me is dear;
But I have lost her through foul play—
Two nights since, she was stol'n away.
2215 Estolt the Proud of Castel Fer
By force of arms hath taken her.
He in his castle keeps her close—
He'll have done with her what he chose.
Such wrath and woe in heart have I
2220 I come indeed right near to die
Of bitter anguish and of grief.
What can I do to find relief?
What comfort can I have, I say,
When all my joy is reft away,
2225 All my delight and all my bliss?
My life a little matter is.
'Tis said, Sir Tristan; If one lose
The one thing that he most would choose,
Then all the rest is nought at all.
2230 Ne'er did such ill-hap me befall,
Therefore I come to you for aid.
You hold all Christendom afraid,
For you are famed the noblest knight
The stoutest and the most upright,
2235 And of all men the greatest lover
That e'er hath been the wide world over;
Therefore your mercy, sir, I cry,
And pray you of your chivalry
You on this quest with me will come
2240 And help me fetch my lover home.
I will your faithful liegeman be
If you herein will stand by me."

Quoth Tristan : " As I may, indeed
Friend, I will help you in this need,
2245 But first to lodging we'll adjourn,
And then set forth upon the morn
And the adventure will assay."
But when he heard him thus delay
He cried in wrath : " Out, friend, for
        shame !
2250 Thou canst not be that knight of fame !
Hadst thou been Tristan, well I know
Thou hadst thyself felt all my woe ;
Tristan has loved so much that he
Well knows what lovers' griefs may be.
2255 If Tristan could have heard my tale
To help my love he could not fail,
To such deep wrong, to such harsh grief
He would not wait to bring relief,
Whate'er thy name may be, good fere,
2260 Thou hast not loved—so much is clear,—
Didst thou know anything of love
I should thy soul to pity move ;
He that knows nought of love, I wis,
Can never know what sorrow is.
2265 And thou, good friend, whose love is
        naught,
Thou canst not feel my grief in aught,
For if thou couldst my sorrows feel
Thou'ldst come with me at my appeal.
Ah, well—I'll go (so God be kind)
2270 Seek the real Tristan till I find ;
He'll comfort me if any may.

Never have I been so astray.
God ! let me die, since I have lost
The thing on earth I loved the most ;
2275 Methinks I were far better dead.
I can no more be comforted,
No more have joy within my soul,
Since I am robbed thus of the whole
Of what in life was lief to me."
2280 Tristan the Dwarf wept piteously,
And was at point to take his leave.
This did the other Tristan grieve,
Who said to him " Fair sir, remain,
For thou by reason hast made plain
2285 That I am bound to go with thee
If I the Lover Tristan be ;
Gladly indeed will I be gone—
Let me but send for arms anon."
He sends for arms and arms for fray,
2290 And with Dwarf Tristan rides away.
Estolt the Proud of Castel Fer
They seek in hope to slay him there.
Still on they ride till by and by
They come unto his castle high.
2295 At a wood's edge they leap from horse
And there await adventure's course.
Estolt the Proud was fierce in fight,
He had six brothers, each a knight,
Hardy and valorous and tall ;
2300 But he in worth outwent them all.
Now two of these from tourney rode ;
Our knights lay hid within the wood

And with a sudden cry leapt out,
Smote them with blows both swift and
    stout,
2305 And the two brothers there fell dead.
The news through all that country sped,
And reached Sir Estolt in due course.
They of the castle sprang to horse,
On the two Tristans straightway bore,
2310 And with stiff strokes assailed them sore.
Right valiant warriors were the twain
Their arms to handle and maintain,
And they held out against them all
Like hardy and skilled knights withal,
2315 And ere the ending of the fight
Four of the foe lay slain outright.
Tristan the Dwarf was smitten through,
The other Tristan wounded too ;
Right through the side and loin, alas !
2320 The lance's venomed point did pass.
Vengeance of wrath he took indeed,
For he slew him that garred him bleed ;
Now are the seven brethren slain,
One Tristan dead, one in sore pain,
2325 For grievous is his body's state.
He gets him home with hardship great
For the fierce anguish he is in,—
Hardly contrives his house to win ;
There they ransack and dress the wound,
2330 And doctors come from all around,
Many and many for his weal.
None of that venom may him heal,

For none perceiveth what it is,
And they are all at fault in this.
2335　They cannot make a salve of worth
To draw or drive the poison forth ;
All day they pluck and pound and grind,
Brew draughts, bray roots and fresh herbs
　　find,
But all their pains are thrown away,
2340　Tristan grows worse from day to day,
The poison spreads throughout his frame,
Within, without, doth all inflame ;
He's black and livid, void of strength,
The bones show through the skin at
　　length.
2345　Now he well sees his life is gone
Save he have instant help anon,
And since no helping hand is nigh
It is right certain he must die ;
His sickness' cure is known of none,
2350　Unless to Queen Iseult alone
His grievous sickness were revealed ;
Were she but with him, he were healed,
But he to her can nowise flee
Through the great hardships of the sea,
2355　Yea, and he dreads that land also,
For he therein has many a foe.
Nor can Iseult to him come over ;
He knows not how he may recover.
All, all his heart is filled with woe,
2360　His weakness weigheth on him so,
With pain and stinking of his wound.

Oft times he wept, oft times he swooned
For anguish of the venomed smart.
Then he called Kaherdin apart,
2365 Thinking to tell him all his need,
For he loved Kaherdin indeed,
And Kaherdin loved him likewise.
He clears the chamber where he lies,
Nor suffers any to remain
2370 Of all the household, save they twain.
Now Iseult marvels in her mind
What thing hereby may be designed—
If from the world he'd be released
And turn to be a monk or priest,
2375 And her whole heart is full of dread.
So by the wall beside his bed,
Outside the room she leans her ear,
All their discourse to overhear,
And posts a servant within call
2380 To watch, while she leans near the wall.
Tristan has so outworn his strength,
That 'gainst the wall he leans at length ;
Kaherdin at his side is set.
Their eyes with piteous tears are wet,
2385 Weeping their fellowship so free
That must be sundered speedily,
Their kindness and their friendship good.
They are full heavy in their mood
With sorrow and with bale and bane ;
2390 The one grieves for the other's pain,
They weep and make great dole of heart
Because their friendship now must part ;

For it was very frank and leal.
Tristan to friendship makes appeal
2395 And saith : " Hear now, sweet friend, I
       pray—
I'm in a strange land far away,
I've here no friend nor any kin
Save thee, sweet comrade Kaherdin ;
Here have I known no peace, no glee,
2400 Save only what I found in thee.
Haply if in my land I were
I might find means to heal me there,
But because here I helpless lie,
Fair, sweet companion, I must die ;
2405 Helpless my death I must endure,
For there is none that can me cure—
Only Queen Iseult hath that skill ;
Yea, she can heal me if she will,
She hath the drug, the power also—
2410 Ay, and the will, could she but know.
I know not what to do, fair friend,
Nor by what means a word to send—
For well I know, were she aware
Of this, she'd aid me by her care
2415 And, by her knowledge, heal my pain.
But how could she come to Bretayn ?
Or could I find a messenger
That would but bear the news to her
She'd comfort me by some wise word
2420 As soon as she my need had heard.
I trust her so, I'll not believe
She would for any hindrance leave

To help me in necessity.
So stedfast is her love to me.
2425   I for myself can nothing do ;
Therefore, sweet friend, I conjure you,
For your great love and kindness' sake,
Pray you, this service undertake !
On my behalf this message bear,
2430   For friendship, for the oath you sware,
And with your hand did seal again,
When Iseult gave you fair Brangwain.
Whereby I pledge my faith to-day,
If you this journey will essay
2435   I will your liegeman ever be
And above all the world, love thee."
Kaherdin looks on Tristan's tears,
His dole and lamentation hears,
His heart is greatly moved thereby,
2440   He answers soft and lovingly,
Saith : " Fair companion, weep not so,
And all thou askest I will do ;
Surely, dear friend, to heal thy sore,
I would me set hard at death's door,
2445   And in great hazard to be slain,
To win some comfort for your pain.
Now by the faith I owe to thee,
It shall not be for lack of me,
Nor aught of my accomplishment,
2450   For anguish nor for strong torment,
That I urge not my power and skill
In everything to do thy will.
Tell me what thou wouldst have her know,

And I'll make ready forth to go."

2455   Tristan replies : " I thank you well !
Now hearken what I have to tell.
Carry away this ring with you,
It is a sign betwixt us two,
And when you come unto the land

2460   Take cloth and silk into your hand,
Seem but a merchant journeying.
Contrive that Iseult see the ring,
For when she hath beheld the stone,
Then will your face to her be known,

2465   And she'll seek art and means whereby
She may speak with you privily.
Then shalt thou bid her hail from me
That hale without her cannot be.
To her I send such hale of heart

2470   That none remaineth for my part.
Say, all my heart for health her haileth,
For in her only health availeth.
All hail that in me is I send her,
Since naught to me can comfort render,

2475   Nor hale of body, nor healing,
Save only such as she can bring.
Save she shall come and make me hale,
Whose lips of comfort cannot fail,
Shall all my health with her remain,

2480   And I die of my bitter pain.
Tell her in brief I am but dead
Save I by her be comforted.
Show her the grief I suffer here,
The weakness and the wound I bear,

2485 And bid her come to comfort me.
Bid her remember verily
The gladness and the dear delight
We had together day and night,
All the great sorrow and distress,
2490 The pleasure and sweet joyousness,
That in our strong true love were found
When in time past she healed my wound,
The drink we drank, both I and she,
That caught us captive on the sea.
2495 For in that draught our death was set,
No comfort may we have of it ;
An ill hour brought that gift about,
It was our death we drank thereout.
Bring to her mind the grief and scorn
2500 That I for love of her have borne :
All, all my kin to me are lost,
The king my uncle and his host ;
I have been banished and reviled
And unto other lands exiled ;
2505 Such woe I've suffered, such travàil
I hardly live and nought avail.
There is no man can ever move
Our great desire and our great love,
Anguish nor sorrow, grief nor dole
2510 Shall never twine us soul from soul ;
The more in those old days they sought
To part us, still the less they wrought ;
Our bodies they had power to sever,
But might not change our loves forever.
2515 Speak of the vow she caused me swear

On that day when I went from her,
Within the garden sundering.
She gave me seisin of the ring,
Bade me, wherever I might dwell,
2520 To love no other woman well.
Nor have I held another dear,
And cannot love thy sister here,
Not she, nor other can me move
While yet the queen has all my love;
2525 So on Iseult my love is set
Your sister is a maiden yet.
Summon her by her faith, and speed
Her hither to me in my need;
Let see if e'er she loved at all!
2530 What else she did for me is small
In worth, if in my bitter strait
She help me not against ill fate.
What shall her friendship now avail
If in my anguish she me fail?
2535 I know not what her love is worth
If she desert me in my dearth,
And little her love profiteth
Save she me succour against death,
And love hath brought me little wealth
2540 If she will help me not to health.
Kaherdin, I know not to say
How strongly for this boon I pray:
Do all thou canst and strive amain,
Greet for me many times Brangwain,
2545 Show her how sore my anguish is:
Save God me help, I'll die of this,

I cannot live for very long
To feel such pain, such torment strong.
Think, friend, to do this happily
2550 And swiftly to return to me,
For save thou come in little space,
Know, thou shalt no more see my face.
I give thee till the fortieth day ;
And if thou do the thing I say,
2555 So that Iseult comes home with you,
Take heed none knows it save we two.
Let not thy sister learn thereof,
Or have suspicion of our love :
Give out it is a cunning wife
2560 Come from afar to save my life.
And thou shalt take my vessel fair,
And place a double sail in her :
One shall be black, the other white ;
And if thou bring Iseult aright,
2565 And if she come to heal my pain,
Sail with the white sail home again,
But if of Iseult thou shouldst lack
Sail hither with the sail of black.
Further to say I do not know ;
2570 May God our Saviour with thee go,
And bring thee safe and sound once more."
He sighs, and groans, and sorrows sore,
And Kaherdin must likewise grieve,
Tristan he's kissed and ta'en his leave,
2575 Prepared for voyage speedily,
And with the first wind puts to sea.
They weigh the anchors, set the sail,

Fleet forward with a gentle gale,
They cleave the waves, they cleave the deep,
2580 They cleave the tall seas and the steep.
And all that noble bachelorhood
Bears silken cloth, and arras good
Broidered with many a wondrous hue.
From Tours were goodly goblets too,
2585 Wine from Poitou, and birds from Spain,
To hide the end he seeks to gain,
Namely, with Queen Iseult to speak
Whom Tristan in his pain doth seek.
His sharp keel cleaves the billows through,
2590 He saileth England's shores unto.
Twenty full days and nights go past
Ere anchor on the isle he cast,
Ere he may come where she doth dwell,
Or even of Iseult hear tell.

2595 Ill is a woman's wrath to dare,
Let every man thereof beware,
For where she loved the best of all
The swiftest will her vengeance fall,
For as their love is lightly won,
2600 Lightly it turns to hate anon,
And longer time endures their wrath,
Once kindled, than their kindness doth.
They know full well their love to bate,
But there's no measure for their hate
2605 When once their anger doth begin.
I dare not speak my mind herein,
'Tis nought to do with me at all.

Iseult was standing by the wall,
And all of Tristan's speech she heard,
2610 Well comprehended every word ;
Now the whole tale of love she knows ;
Great wrath within her bosom glows
Because her heart for Tristan yearned
While he toward another turned.
2615 But now is everything made plain
Why she no joy in him may gain.
Well she remembers all she's heard,
But makes pretence to know no word ;
Yet, at the first chance she shall see
2620 She will avenge her cruelly
On what on earth she loveth most.
Soon as the doors were all unclosed
Iseult into the chamber steals,
Her wrath from Tristan she conceals,
2625 Serves him and shows him semblance sweet
As is from love to lover meet ;
Full tenderly with him she speaks,
And often goes to kiss his cheeks,
And shows him love and semblance kind
2630 But all the while in wrathful mind
Thinks how her vengeance may be wrought.
And many a time she asked and sought
When Kaherdin should come again
Bringing the leech to heal his pain.
2635 Yet no true pity in her bides.
Close in her heart the crime she hides,
Resolved to do it if she may,
For anger so her mind doth sway.

Kaherdin sails across the sea,
2640 Nor of his sailing ceaseth he
Till to the land he cometh in
Whither he goes to seek the queen :
That is, unto the mouth of Thames ;
So sails up with his silks and gems.
2645 For in Thames mouth, without the bar,
In port his anchors casten are,
And in his boat he makes voyage
To London, under London Bridge,
His merchandise displayeth there,
2650 Folds and outspreads the silk cloths fair.

London's a right rich city free,
Better is none in Christentie,
None worthier, none more filled with
    praise,
Furnished with folk that dwell at ease.
2655 Lovers of honour and largesse,
They live in full great joyousness.
The very heart of England's there,
You need not seek it otherwhere.
There Thames runs by beneath the wall,
2660 Where pass the merchant vessels all,
From every land both high and low,
Where Christian merchants come and go.
There men full wise and cunning bin,
And thither comes Dan Kaherdin,
2665 With all his birds, with all his stuff,
That are full good and fair enough.
He takes a great hawk on his wrist,

And a cloth where wondrous colours twist,
Likewise a cup most finely wrought,
2670 Chased and enamelled in fair sort.
These to King Mark he doth present,
And courteous saith—With this intent
He with his goods to London drew
That he might add fresh stores thereto ;
2675 Therefore he prays for the king's peace,
That through the land none may him seize,
And he no loss nor shame sustain
At hand of count nor chamberlain.
Sure peace on him the king bestows,
2680 As his whole household hears and knows.
To the queen's chamber next he hies
To show her of his merchandise.
A clasp well wrought of finest gold
Kaherdin in his hand doth hold,
2685 The world hath not its like, I trow.
This on the queen he doth bestow :
" The gold of it is good," saith he,
Better did Iseult never see.
He takes from finger Tristan's ring,
2690 Sets it beside the other thing,
And says : " I pray thee, queen, behold,
This is a better coloured gold
Than even this ring, which yet, look you,
I deem a right good jewel too."
2695 Now when Iseult the ring had seen,
She looked, and straight knew Kaherdin,
Her colour changed, her heart did leap,
And she sighed much for anguish deep.

That here were tidings well she knew.
2700 So Kaherdin aside she drew,
Asked if the ring were to be sold,
And what its price might be in gold,
And had he other merchandise ?
All this she does in cunning wise
2705 That she her guards might clean outwit.
When Kaherdin alone did sit
With Iseult : " Hearken, dame," said he,
" My words, and mark them carefully.
Tristan doth send, as lover true,
2710 His greeting, service, love to you,
As to his lady and his love
In whom his life and death do move.
He is your vassal and your friend ;
I on his errand hither wend
2715 To say, he can have comfort none
Of death, unless by you alone,
No hope of life, and no healing
Save only such as you may bring.
He with a lance was hurt to death
2720 Whose poisoned point envenometh,
And nowhere may we find a leech
Whose drugs have skill his hurt to reach ;
So many have made trial and lacked,
His wretched body is all racked,
2725 He languishes and lives in dole,
With stinking wounds and grief of soul.
He lets you know, he cannot live
Save only you your succour give ;
Whom thus by me he summoneth,

2730 And calls upon you by that faith,
And by the loyal trust and true
To him, Iseult, at your hand due,
You shall not for this world forgo
To come away to him right so.

2735 Never before was such sharp need,
Therefore thou canst not not give heed.
Remember that great tenderness,
And all the sorrows and distress
That you and he together tasted.

2740 His life and youth are wholly wasted,
Yea for your sake he has been banned,
Many times driven from the land,
King Mark his uncle is his foe :
O think how much he bare of woe !

2745 Let you remember of the oath
That was at parting 'twixt you both,
When in the garden you embraced ;
Then on his hand this ring you placed
And promised him your love also.

2750 Some pity, lady, to him show !
For save you will some succour yield,
Certes, he never will be healed ;
Without you he cannot recover,
And it behoves you to come over,

2755 Since otherwise he cannot live.
Thus faithfully his words I give.
He sends this ring as token true,
Keep it—it is his gift to you."
Now when Iseult his message learned

2760 Great anguish in her bosom burned,

And pain and grief and pity sad,
Worse than she ever yet had had.
Deeply she broods and much she sighs,
And all her soul for Tristan cries,
2765   But knows not how she may him seek.
Then with Brangwain she goes to speak,
She tells her all the story clear :
The wound made by the venomed spear,
The pain he bears, the agony,
2770   And how he languishing must lie ;
How and by whom he asks her aid,
Else whole he never may be made ;
And when these griefs are all made known
Takes counsel what may now be done.
2775   And now begins the mighty sighing,
And the complaining and the crying,
And pain and heaviness of soul,
The grieving and the bitter dole
They made while they together spake,
2780   Being so sorry for his sake.
Natheless, such counsel and such speech
They hold, as this resolve to reach,
That they for journey will prepare
And straight with Kaherdin forth fare,
2785   On Tristan's pain their skill to try
In this his great necessity.
To start at nightfall they're agreed,
Make ready all the things they need.
When other folk are all asleep
2790   In stealthy wise by night they creep,
By cunning and good fortune great,

Forth at a little postern gate
Which lookèd out upon Thames side ;
The stream was high with the flood tide.
2795 There was a boat all ready kept
And into it Queen Iseult stept.
Then with the ebb they drive and sail
And quickly flee before the gale.
They strain each nerve with speed to go,
2800 And never cease to sail and row
Until by the great ship they lie.
They hoist the sail and forth they fly.
Fast as the wind may drive them on
They fleet the long sea-ways upon ;
2805 Skirting the coast of that strange land
They passed, and Wissant harbour scanned,
Past Boulogne and Treport they go.
The favouring winds behind them blow.
Their light ship answers readily
2810 The helm, they pass by Normandy ;
Gaily they sail with gladsome mind,
For the strong gales to them are kind.

Tristan who lies in deadly anguish,
Now in his bed doth grieve and languish ;
2815 Of nothing can he comfort win,
He gets no good of medicine,
Nought he may do may bring him aid,
His whole hope is on Iseult stayed,
He hath no will for anything,
2820 Nought, save Iseult, can pleasure bring,
He, but for her, were long since dead ;

He wastes and waits there in his bed,
He lives in hope she may come to him,
And heal his sickness and renew him,
2825 Knows, if she fail him, life is o'er.
All day he sends down to the shore
To see if chance the ship returns ;
No other thought within him burns.
Often he bids them carry him
2830 And make his bed by the sea's brim,
To watch and see his vessel come,
How and with what sail sailing home.
He takes no thought for anything
Save only for that home-coming.
2835 For all his heart this hope doth fill,
All his desire and all his will ;
All that he hath seems void and dim
Unless the queen will come to him.
And oft he bids them bear him back,
2840 So many doubts his spirit rack,
Because he fears she cometh not
And that she hath her faith forgot ;
Better from others hear about her
Than see the ship come in without her.
2845 Tristan to see the ship doth yearn,
Yet failure cannot bear to learn :
Thus his whole heart is full of pain,
Yet of the sight he is most fain.
Oft to his wife his woes he speaks,
2850 Yet will not tell her what he seeks,
Save Kaherdin that comes no more.
So long he stays, he feareth sore

His venture never will succeed.

Hear now a piteous hap indeed,
2855 And an adventure sorrowful,
To every lover pitiable !
Of so much love, of such desire,
Ne'er have ye heard a dole more dire.
Where Tristan for Iseult doth wait
2860 Thither the lady saileth straight,
And quickly comes quite close to land.
As soon as they behold the strand
Then are they glad and gaily sail.
But from the south there springs a gale
2865 Smites from before the sail spread out,
And turns the whole ship round about,
They haste to luff, they turn the sail,
Howe'er they strive, they can't prevail,
The wind grows fierce, the waves awake,
2870 And the deep sea begins to quake ;
Storm lowers ; the air is thick with wrack,
The billows lift, the sea grows black,
Rain, hail and storm from worse to worst
Grow ; the shrouds crack, the bowlines
      burst ;
2875 They strike the sail ; the vessel rides
Driving at will of winds and tides.
Their boat was lowered long before,
When they were close to their own shore ;
Alas ! they had forgotten it,
2880 And a wave smote it bit from bit ;
Not only have they lost thus much,

But wind and storm are risen to such,
No sailor, be he ne'er so feat,
Can stand at all upon his feet.
2885 All weep aloud, and all complain,
And all for fear are in great pain.
Then said Iseult : " Ah, me, poor wretch !
God wills not that my life should stretch
So far, Tristan my love to see,
2890 But wills that I be drowned at sea.
Had I spoke first with thee, then I,
Tristan, should little reck to die.
Fair love, when thou shalt know me dead
Thou never shalt be comforted.
2895 Thou for my death shalt feel such woe,
Being already brought so low,
That healèd shalt thou never be.
My coming rests not now with me ;
I had been with you, by God's will,
2900 And set myself to search your ill ;
For now no other grief have I
But that thou must unholpen lie.
This is the grief, and this the dole
That makes me heavy in my soul :
2905 That thou hast nought which comforteth
Thee, if I die, against thy death.
For my own death I care no whit,
If God wills it, then I will it ;
But when thou hear'st it presently
2910 I know that thou thereof wilt die.
Such is the love between us two
I cannot suffer but through you,

You cannot die without me, friend,
Nor I, without you, make an end.
2915 Must I at sea in peril go,
Then you ought to be drowned also.
On land you cannot drownèd be,
You've come to seek me on the sea ;
I see your death before my eye,
2920 And know that soon I too must die.
Love ! my desire is set at nought !
To die within your arms I thought,
And in one tomb my burial win ;
But now we have quite failed herein.
2925 Nay, even so it might come round,
For if I needs must here be drowned,
And you too, as I dream, drowned thus,
One fish might swallow both of us ;
And on this fashion we might come,
2930 Perchance, fair friend, to have one tomb,
For we might be some good man's prize
Who should our bodies recognise,
And with such lofty honour serve
As our great love doth well deserve.
2935 It never can be as I say !
God willing, it might chance that way.
What shouldst thou seek at sea, sweet fere ?
I wot not what thou shouldst do here.
But here am I, and here shall drown,
2940 Without thee, heart, to death go down.
By this I'm softly comforted ;
Fair love, thou ne'er wilt know I'm dead,
None shall hear of it, far from here—

I know not who should tell thee, dear.
2945 Thou shalt live long time after me,
Still looking I should come to thee,
And, if God will, grow hale and strong;
Above all else, for this I long;
Healing for thee I covet more
2950 E'en than I long to reach the shore,
Such utter love to thee I bear.
Yet, O my love, must I feel fear
Lest, thou being healed, when I am dead
I be no more rememberèd;
2955 I dead, thou living, thou shalt find
Another woman to thy mind.
Iseult at least, the white-hand maid,
Tristan, I doubt, and am afraid.
Ought I to doubt?   I know not, I;
2960 But if before me you should die
I should live short time after you.
I nothing know what I should do,
But above all I want thee, sweet.
God grant we may together meet,
2965 That to thy pain I bring relief,
Or we two die of this one grief!"

Thus, while the tempest still remains,
Iseult laments her and complains.
Five days and more beat lustily
2970 Storm and foul weather on the sea,
Till the sun shines, and falls the gale.
Then up they hoist the snow-white sail,
Swift scudding, till Kaherdin's eye

The coasts of Brittany doth spy.
2975   Then are they glad and full of glee,
And spread their canvas merrily,
So that far off 'tis plain to sight
Which sail it is, the black or white;
Far off its hue they would display,
2980   For know, this was the latest day
Tristan had set for their return
Since they had left their country's bourne.
But while with merry cheer they sail
The heat comes up and the winds fail,
2985   That sail they cannot in no wise;
Quite smooth and full the ocean lies,
This way nor that the ship can stir
But as the wave may carry her,
And they have no boat any more:
2990   Thus is their anguish very sore,
For close before them lies the strand,
Where, without wind, they cannot land,
Now up a-top, and now below,
They toss and tumble to and fro,
2995   And in this fashion make no way;
Great is their trouble and dismay.
Much torment hath Iseult, to see
The land she longs for ardently
And yet in no wise may attain;
3000   She is nigh dead for eager pain.
All in the ship desire the shore,
But still too soft the breeze drifts o'er;
And wailing is on Iseult's lip.
They on the shore desire the ship,

3005 But still they stretch their eyes in vain.
Therefore is Tristan in deep pain,
Full oft he weeps, full oft he sighs,
And his whole heart for Iseult cries
With body tost, and salt tears shed,
3010 And for great longing well-nigh dead.
Amid this anguish and great strife
Before him comes Iseult his wife,
A cunning plot her mind within,
And saith : " Friend, here comes Kaherdin ;
3015 I've seen his ship come sailing free,
Scarce yet in sight, across the sea,
Yet well enough I saw, to know
It is his ship comes sailing so ;
God grant such news he may bring in
3020 That you at heart may comfort win ! "
Then at that word Tristan upstart,
And cried to Iseult : " Fair, sweet heart,
Is that his ship, his, without fail ?
Tell me, what colour is the sail ? "
3025 Then said Iseult : " In sooth, alack !
Know that the sail is all of black,
And hoist aloft, and high outspread
Because the wind is slack and dead."
Such bitter dole had Tristan then
3030 As ne'er hath been, nor shall again,
So to the wall he turned his head :
" God save Iseult and me," he said,
" For if thou wilt not come to me,
Then I must die for love of thee ;
3035 I can no more, my life must end,

For thee I die, Iseult, sweet friend ;
Thou hast no pity for my pain,
Yet by my death thy tears I'll gain ;
Love, this makes me a little glad,
3040 That thou for my death wilt be sad.
True love Iseult," three times he said,
And at the fourth time he was dead.

Throughout the house was weeping then
Of knights and peers and noblemen,
3045 Loud their complaint and shrill their
    cries.
The warriors and the knights arise,
Bear out his body from the bed,
Set it on cloth of samite spread,
And with a pall of colours veil.
3050 Then on the sea upsprings the gale ;
It strikes the bellying sail within,
And to the land the ship brings in.
Out of the ship Iseult steps down,
Hears the great clamour in the town,
3055 From church and chapel hears the bell :
" What news ? " she bids the townsmen
    tell,
Wherefore the tolling is so great,
Wherefore all eyes with tears are wet.
Then said an ancient man and grave :
3060 " Fair dame, as God me see and save,
Great grief is fallen on us all,
As never folk did worse befall.
Tristan is dead, the brave, the free ;

Great comfort to this realm was he ;
3065 He to the poor was generous,
And helpful to the dolorous,
Of a deep wound within his side
He in his bed just now has died ;
Never before so deep distress
3070 Came all this kingdom to oppress."
When that Iseult the news had heard,
For grief she could not speak one word ;
For Tristan's sake so great her woes,
Bareheaded through the streets she goes
3075 Before them to the palace door.
Truly the Bretons ne'er before
Had seen a woman half so fair.
Through all the town they marvel where
Her home may be, and what her name.
3080 Then to the body Iseult came,
And turning to the eastward she
Made prayer for him most piteously :
" Since I behold thee dead, sweet friend,
I too of life must make an end ;
3085 All for my love thou comest to die,
And I die, love, for misery,
Because in time I could not come
To heal thee of thy evil doom.
Love, love, for this the death of thee
3090 Nothing can ever comfort me,
Delight, nor mirth, nor any joy.
God's hate that evil storm destroy.
That on the sea so long me stayed,
I could not come, friend, to thy aid !

3095 Wherefore must I too late attain?
I would have brought you life again,
And spoken tenderly with you
Of that love which was 'twixt us two,
And made complaint of all our fate:
3100 The joyousness and pleasure great,
The bitter pain and dolorous,
Which love hath alway brought to us.
All this had I brought back to mind,
And clipped and kissed you and been
     kind.
3105 Since I might heal thee not, God send
We now together make an end!
Since I in time came not aright,
Nor knew not of thy evil plight,
But found death waiting overseas,
3110 Of that same draught will I have ease.
Thy life is lost because of me,
And I will thy true leman be,
And will to die for thee likewise."
She kisses him and down she lies,
3115 And kisses both his mouth and face,
And very closely doth embrace;
Mouth upon mouth and breast to breast
Straightway her spirit findeth rest;
Close at his side she dieth thus
3120 For lover's grief most piteous.
Sir Tristan died for longing great,
Iseult because she came too late,
All for love's sake did Tristan die,
And Fair Iseult for misery.

3125 Here Thomas brings to end the tale,
Here he bids all true lovers hail,
The dolorous, the amorous,
The envious, the valorous,
The joyous and the frenzied—all
3130 Upon whose ears the tale shall fall.
Though here they find not all their will
I did the best with my poor skill,
And the whole truth I have rehearsed
As I made promise at the first.
3135 I wrought the story and the rime
As an example to all time,
That I the tale might beautify
And please all lovers' hearts thereby,
So that they find in every part
3140 Matter to give them greater heart.
May they draw comfort from my song
Against all change, against all wrong,
Against all tears, all griefs that move,
And against all the wiles of love.

The End of the Romance of Tristan.

*Printed and Made in Great Britain by The Crypt House Press Limited,
Gloucester and London*

BENN'S ESSEX LIBRARY

(Already published, continued from facing title).

THE DRAMA OF THE LAW
    By SIR EDWARD PARRY

AN OUTCAST OF THE ISLANDS
    By JOSEPH CONRAD

MR. TEDDY
    By E. F. BENSON

THE LAND OF HEART'S DESIRE AND THE
    COUNTESS CATHLEEN
    By W. B. YEATS

SISTER TERESA
    By GEORGE MOORE

SONGS OF A SOURDOUGH
    By ROBERT W. SERVICE

TRISTAN IN BRITTANY
    Translated by DOROTHY L. SAYERS, M.A.
    With an Introduction by GEORGE SAINTSBURY

THE STORY OF AN AFRICAN FARM
    By OLIVE SCHREINER

Other titles will be announced from time to time.

Ernest Benn Limited, Bouverie House, Fleet Street, E.C. 4